Why Do My Employees Hate Me

AND OTHER ANSWERS YOU MAY NOT WANT TO HEAR.

William J Eisenbrandt

Dedication

To Casey, who made it possible for me to put this book together

and

To Dylan, who inspired me to take action and create something that could help small business owners keep their doors open

Contents

Acknowledgment ix

    Why We Are All Here. xi

1   Why Do My Employees Hate Me? 1

2   Why Doesn't Anything Ever Get Done On Time? 9

3   Why Does It Feel Like My Company Never Gains
    Any Momentum? 15

4   Why Are We Losing Customers? 25

5   Why Is Our Competition Growing While We Struggle
    To Survive? 41

6   Why Can't My Employees Get Along With
    Each Other? 49

7   Why Do We Spend So Much On Advertising And
    Get So Little In Return? 57

8   Why Is Our Entire Marketing Budget Focused
    On Something Called Brand Awareness? 63

9   What Is The Most Important Asset My
    Company Owns? 71

10   Why Can't My Sales Team Sell Anything? 77

11   Why Do We Have To Mark Everything Down
    Before We Can Sell It? 83

12   Why Can't We Hire Anyone Good? 89

13 Why Are We Wasting Time On Projects That
Have Nothing To Do With Our Business?.................. 97

14 Why Are All The Good Ideas Already Taken?.............. 103

15 Why Is Everyone Telling Me Social Media
Is Important?.. 113

16 Why Are My Costs Going Through The Roof?............ 119

17 Why Do We Have Such Bad Luck?...................... 125

18 How Do I Get My Employees To Stop Making
Mistakes?... 135

19 Why Can't Anyone Make A Marketing Brochure
That Works?.. 141

20 Why Can't I Get Support From Local Businesses? 151

21 When Will Things Settle Down So I Can Finally
Grow My Business?.................................. 159

22 When Will I Ever Be Able To Step Back And Let My Business
Support Me Instead Of The Other Way Around?........... 167

23 I've Got It All Figured Out............................ 173

Dear Reader

This book contains several suggestions for you and your business. While these suggestions are based on the experiences of the author, every business is different, and the results of your actions can vary widely.

The author is not in the business of providing legal, accounting, financial, or other professional service advice. Before making any changes to your business or life, please seek out the advice of competent professionals in these areas.

Acknowledgments

In my professional career I have come across a wide range of people in management positions. I have seen the great, the good, the OK, the "what were you thinking," and the awful. In my own management career I know I aspired to being in the good-to-great category and at times found myself struggling to reach that ideal. The truth is, management is tough. Leadership is tough. Business ownership is nearly impossible to do well, and too often we take for granted the efforts of these leaders and see them through the lenses of our own cynicism.

I want to acknowledge all of the managers, leaders, business owners, and coworkers, both good and bad, who have shaped my experiences and knowledge of business. This book could not have been written without the lessons you taught me.

WHY WE ARE ALL HERE

I was never good at being an employee.

I grew up in a house where businesses were launched frequently. I knew in the sixth grade that I was going to run my own business. We were given a project where we had to find a job in the want ads and then pretend to live for a month off that salary. I went straight to the teacher and told him I couldn't find my job in the paper. When he asked what I was looking for, I said, "CEO." He turned around and walked back to his desk shaking his head. The next day he picked my job for me.

After graduating from high school, I found that every job I did get was boring. I didn't have the education to get into a real "profession" so I was stuck in service-related jobs. The pay was low, the work was repetitive, and I was miserable. About every five to six months, I'd change jobs just because I was sure the grass was actually greener. What I found, though, is that if the grass really was greener it was because of all the manure that came flowing from the managers.

I spent several years moving from job to job, industry to industry, trying to see if I had the unfortunate luck of a few bad bosses or if this was actually normal. I was disappointed to find that even good companies had bad managers, bad leaders, even bad business owners. And this thought occurred to me: maybe it really is me and not them. So I decided if I was going to make things better, I needed to further my education. Whether or not I was the problem, I wasn't going to let my education (or lack thereof) be an excuse. And besides, I was tired of all the crap jobs. I wanted something more substantial, something where I could make a difference. Several degrees and different advanced learning programs later, I was ready to take on the corporate world.

When I finally broke into the professional space, it wasn't much better. There were too many rules and too many rule makers. I had bosses who made it obvious their entire goal was to enforce the rules rather than to focus on the success or failure of the business. And I took the time to point out just how meaningless their actions really were. Since when did all these stupid rules have anything to do with growing a business?

I saw myself as a bold go-getter, young and ambitious enough to challenge the status quo and bring forth a new era of corporate greatness. But mostly I was perceived as a spoiled brat who didn't know his place. Over and over I was told, "You're young and naïve. You'll figure this out eventually, and then you'll thank me for trying to help you now." And that was usually followed by a laundry list of "duties" that were designed to remind me about my place in the corporate structure (you know scrub the toilets, sit in the corner, don't talk to anyone—it was like being punished in kindergarten).

That's when I realized I'm just not meant to be an employee. I've been self-employed ever since as a small business consultant. My experiences had taught me that even with a great product or service, small businesses that run poorly struggle to survive. My education in marketing, accounting, finance, and business operations all taught me that nothing is more important to a business than generating revenue. So when I started my consulting firm, I zeroed in on all these businesses that just seemed to have lost focus on what was important. They needed the wakeup call that says it's not really about the rules, it's about the survival of your business. Trust me, I learned the hard way that it is not really an easy sell—"Hey, your business sucks; it could be better, but you don't know what the hell you are doing, so hire me and I'll fix it all for you." Of course, I used much more flowery language than that, but it was a waste of time. I would have gotten just as far by saying that.

They say it's lonely at the top. There are so few business owners out there, and even fewer who are willing to share their experiences with others. Sometimes, as a business owner, you can feel like there is no one to turn to when you need to talk through a problem. It's almost impossible to find a sounding board you can trust when you are trying to come up with a new strategy. My role as a consultant is to fill those needs. This book is a collection of the most common problems I have seen with small businesses.

Through my experiences, I eventually came to two conclusions about decision makers in small businesses. The first conclusion is that they rarely hear the truth about their business. If the business is big enough to have employees, they are reluctant to have a frank and honest conversation with the boss. There are a lot of reasons for this: fear they will lose their job, loyalty to the employee who screwed up, or they just flat out don't care either way, to name a few. But the fact remains the same: bad news is hidden or softened, and good news is spread far and wide (and exaggerated, just a bit).

The only true feedback decision makers get is from customer complaints. But even this is exaggerated a bit. The only time customers really complain is when they think it will help them get their way. Since the majority of really upset customers tend to simply leave and never come back, the complaints that do come through aren't taken too seriously. And what's even sadder is that most complaints get round filed before anyone ever takes a moment to question if there is a problem with the business process that caused this customer to be unhappy.

The second conclusion I discovered about decision makers is that they aren't equipped to handle the truth. Cue Jack Nicholson from *A Few Good Men*—"You can't handle the TRUTH." Because these decision makers have been coddled by their employees and customers, they have a skewed impression of what their business is really doing. It's also why so often business owners tend to overreact when they do discover something negative about their company. They are like proud parents finding out their child is flunking a class or has started smoking. It's not just the problem that gets them; it's the overriding shock that makes it so difficult.

As a consultant, I use these truths to my advantage. I am honest and direct with all of my clients. If you ask me a question, I am not going to consider your feelings or your mental state before answering. I'm not going to use flowery language to help you feel better about the answer. I used to, but then I realized being nice about it just perpetuated the problem. Nope, with me you are going to get the straight (sometimes painful, almost always offensive) truth, and then it is up to you to decide what you are going to do with it.

This is difficult for even the most secure business owner. All of us like to think that even with all our faults we are still doing the right things most of the time. It's hard to hear someone saying that the problems you are facing are because of mistakes you made. It's even harder to take a step back and accept what is being said or even going so far as to believe it really is the truth. But once we accept the truth about ourselves and our businesses, we have a chance to make the decisions that will bring about change.

Running a business is hard enough without playing word games. Every time I ask a question, I keep track of how many words it took to get the answer. The more words used, the farther from the truth this answer is getting. I hate answers that include "ifs" and "buts." If you do nothing else, simply making your employees answer your questions in ten words or less will give you a clearer picture of your business.

This book is the straight truth based on my experience. I'm not going to beat around the bush with any of the answers to these questions. And just to be clear, these aren't the questions I typically get asked. I get asked silly questions like "how do we maximize our ROI" or "what is the next marketing paradigm shift we should prepare for?" It's like somebody read an article full of buzzwords and decided to cram them into a question. These are the same questions a person asks who is more interested in what time a salesperson showed up at the office rather than whether or not he closed a new deal. In other words, these are the wrong questions. This book is a good start on the right questions you should be asking.

Now all you have to do is decide if you are ready to accept that you really don't have the whole story on your business.

If you are ready to accept that what you know about your business might just be a mirage, then you are ready for the rest of this book. If you think you can handle the cold, hard truths, then follow me on this journey. I'm about to tell you why your business sucks, how you screwed it up, and how you need my advice to get it fixed.

Ready?

1

Why Do My Employees Hate Me?

In Short, Because You're A Jackass!

A ren't you glad you turned the page? I have never met a person ambitious enough to start a business and keep it running more than five years who doesn't have a little jackass in them. It's part of your DNA, and it is what gives you the edge you need to take risks and be successful. But your drive and passion for your business aren't why your employees hate you.

Your employees are struggling to pay their bills each month. But they get to hear about how awful your weekend was because your spouse spent all day Saturday buying a new car and you couldn't get out on the boat. You talk about how last year your vacation in the Bahamas wasn't very good because of the weather while your employees use their time off for when they are sick.

You talk about how the working class doesn't understand the pressures of running a business. Your employees watch you buy artwork for the office one day and get upset the next because someone is wasting paper by printing off a thirty-page document.

You are inconsistent with your praise when things go well. When things are bad, you spread the blame to the nearest person. Owning a business is tough, both financially and emotionally. But you are taking it out on those who support you.

They hate you because you care about your business more than you care about them. They hate you because you are more successful than they are. They hate you because you keep them from living their dreams. They hate you because they need someone to blame.

"But I'm providing these people a job, money, security, benefits, and training. What more do they want from me, my blood? I can't believe how ungrateful these people are. I should get rid of them all if they don't want to work for me." This was the response by one business owner when I told him his employees resented working for him.

Every time he tried to prove he was a good boss and a generous employer, he proved that he was a jackass. He accused his employees of being lazy and doing just enough to get the job done and nothing more. We walked around, and he saw a couple of employees talking in a hall. "See that? They're stealing from me. Right there in front of me, taking my money and doing nothin'." It doesn't matter what you say in public; if you feel this way about your employees in private, you are going to be seen as a jackass!

You could say you don't give a second thought to what your employees think of you. You could stay in denial and truly believe the problem lies with your employees and not with you. But that's a victim mentality, and I won't ever let a business owner get away with it. You made the choice to be an ass, you made the choice to treat these people like that, you made the choice to bring in people who don't care about your business—now live with it or fix it.

The old ways of running a business with an iron fist and having loyal, dedicated followers is gone forever. We have entered a new era in social responsibility. The new generation coming into the workforce is idealistic and highly focused on perceived fairness. And not just fairness in how they are treated, but fairness in how the company treats society, the environment, customers, vendors, the community, and just about anything else that could be potentially touched by you.

Quite the responsibility for one business owner to shoulder.

You can certainly brush this off and continue business as usual, but it doesn't change the fact that corporate citizenship is now sitting front and center in your employees' minds.

When you made the decision to hire an employee, you agreed to many things: hours, wage, benefits, working conditions, etc. What you may not be aware of is that there was an unspoken agreement that you and your employee entered into. You expected this employee to work hard and sacrifice. Your employee expected you to work hard and sacrifice. The moment either of you appear selfish to the other, that contract is broken and the trust between you is gone.

When your employees break this deal, you remove them from your business. But when you break it, your employees don't leave. Not immediately anyway. They sit and they stew. They share their mistrust with others. Soon everyone knows you are selfish, and no one wants to work for you. Bottom line: your employees hate you, and in order to keep your business moving forward, you are going to need to start thinking about the relationships you and your business are nurturing.

I'd like to say that companies that try to do good and make the right choices always end up successful in the end. That the evil companies that are selfish and exploit others always end up failing. But we know that isn't true. Those are stories that belong in fairy tales and in Hollywood. But I am working to change that. One of my big vision goals is to help entrepreneurs build strong businesses that are focused on the principle of "do no harm."

Before doctors can treat a patient, they agree to some form of the original Hippocratic oath. Over time, that oath has been modified to incorporate the changes in medicine and in our society. In that oath, in one form or another, they state they will treat those that are sick to the best of their ability and to do no harm. The "do no harm" clause exists all the way back to the original Greek translation. Why would it survive for so many years when so much of our "honor" culture has faded?

I'll get to that answer soon. Next let's look at financial planners and public accountants. Each of these professions is required to agree to a standardized code of ethics. In the code of ethics for certified public accountants, article 2, clause 53.04 states:

All who accept membership in the American Institute of Certified Public Accountants commit themselves to honor the public trust. In return for the faith that the public reposes in them, members should seek continually to demonstrate their dedication to professional excellence.

It's a fancy way of saying, "Do no harm."

What do doctors, financial planners, and accountants have in common? They have a unique and distinctive set of skills and knowledge. With that knowledge, they rely on the trust of their clients in order to perform their services. If the profession loses the faith of the public (think: attorneys and car salesmen), their entire industry suffers.

Imagine going to work tomorrow with the weight of your profession on your shoulders. A doctor has to make the right decision every time. Not just for his honor, not just for the sake of the patient, but for the honor of the entire profession and the sake of every future patient. What would happen if the public could no longer trust doctors or nurses?

We dealt with a crisis of faith in the banking industry during 2008 and 2009 when the financial markets started to shut down. We had another crisis of faith in the auto industry when General Motors declared bankruptcy and had to get a "loan" from the federal government just to keep the doors open. How long does it take to rebuild that trust?

Now think of the average small business owner. Do you think the public holds business owners closer to the ideals of doctors or to those of Wall Street insiders? As a small business owner, you travel a path right down the middle of that road. What are you doing to improve the perception people have about you and your business? Thinking about what you stand for and what you believe in is going to have a large effect on your decision making and ultimately on the direction of your business.

Every action and every decision you make are a reflection on you. If you want to grow your business, you will need the support of all your stakeholders. Stakeholders include your customers, your potential customers, your suppliers, your vendors, your employees, your family, your community, and even people who will never have anything to do with you. It doesn't mean you have to be a nice person, but it does mean you have to treat others with respect.

When you decide to double park, it reflects on your character. No one cares about the emergency you were taking care of that caused you to park like that. The public is unforgiving, and they remember every poor decision or hurtful action you take. Just like in our childhood stories about honor, it is your reputation and the reputation of your business that is on the line every day. Respect the power of your decisions.

What I have found is that anyone who feels they have been wronged, whether they are a customer, a vendor, an employee or just a random bystander, will talk about it. They are going to tell their family and friends. They are going to tell friends of friends. They are going to tell coworkers and other customers. They are going to walk up to strangers and tell them, too. When you treat someone well, they are going to talk about it, but only to their friends and family. They aren't going to spend much more time than that on it. It's why bad news always seems to spread faster than good news. Knowing that, you need to make a conscious effort to turn yourself and your business into a good corporate citizen if you ever want to build positive momentum.

Entrepreneurs, especially successful entrepreneurs, have a bit of a self-ish streak in them. OK, I'll lighten up a bit and call it being selfish rather than being a jackass. But some people will say business owners have an unhealthy obsession with their dream, and that might even be a better description. In order to build a business, they have to work more than just a forty-hour week. It means less time for family and friends. The stress of keeping the business successful means that the business owner can't always be liked in the office. Being a business owner can be a lonely experience.

Without a healthy respect for others, business owners run the risk of alienating many of the stakeholders they rely on. By focusing so internally on you and your dream, you miss out on the needs of others. There are two questions I tell all of my clients they need to remember:

How often are you looking for ways to help others be successful?

How often do you set others up to be successful?

The first question is about expanding your horizons. We so often look at situations in terms of how we can benefit personally. Our cynicism keeps us from stretching too far, so if we can't immediately benefit we discard the offer and move on. But a person who is looking to build meaningful relationships is always looking for ways to help others. Take each situation that comes to you and look at it from more than one perspective. Try to find a way to use that situation to create an opportunity for someone else you know.

The second question is about how often you act on the behalf of others. It's not enough to scan the horizon for opportunities. When you see something that can help someone you know, are you taking the time to explore it and offer it up to your network?

When you elevate someone else, you are reinforcing a positive image of yourself and your business. What does a positive image do for you?

First of all, it creates positive word of mouth. I've heard many business owners say that they get most of their clientele from positive word of mouth. Secondly, by helping another person or business out, you are creating a stronger alliance that will pay dividends down the road. This person may never buy from you, but they may look to repay that kindness by finding opportunities for you.

In a more personal way, when you help others, your mindset and emotions will start to change. It can give you a new perspective about how your business operates. When you take stock of your customers, you will have ideas on how to serve them better. You will get ideas on how to keep your employees more engaged and focused on the vision of the company. In short, by giving of yourself, you improve your leadership skills and the relationships you have with everyone in your company.

Now take a hard look at your past behavior. Are you building up a positive image, or are you confirming the negative image most people want to believe about people in power? Everything you see and experience in your business is a direct result of your actions. It can be hard to face the truth about your actions. You can take the long, hard road and try to lay blame at everyone else's feet. But eventually you will have to accept that you made these decisions, and it was based on those decisions that your company is struggling and your employees hate you. The sooner you come to this realization the better—because you can't fix something until you are willing to admit that it is broken!

The unfortunate truth is that all it takes is one small slight to create mistrust in an organization. I have seen salespeople lose all confidence in their abilities simply because a business owner interrupted a sales call and took over the meeting in order to close the deal. The business owner sees it as a closed deal and moves on. The salesperson sees it as a sign that no one trusts him to close a deal. The next sale is a little harder because the salesperson is now looking over his shoulder and wondering if he is really qualified to make a deal. This is how morale turns and you start being seen as a jackass.

The peaks and valleys of a business can sometimes require a business owner to cut costs. In extreme circumstances, the company may be forced to lay off staff. Even though these actions are a necessity for the overall health of the business, many of your employees and customers won't understand why the staff has to be reduced. The result is unhappy customers because there aren't enough service people to take orders or answer calls. Employees are uneasy because now they don't trust that their position is secure anymore.

What's worse is when the cost cutting happens because of a poor management decision. It can be hard to predict the future, but in business it is a requirement to try. You have to predict reasonably what the market is going to need, how much of it the market will need, how you will deliver it, and how much people will pay for it. Get any of those wrong, and you could be considerably under or over staffed. Either way you run the risk of having a negative opinion build up in the organization.

Now these are examples of ways you could inadvertently create a negative image of yourself. There are untold numbers of ways you can do it intentionally. I don't know why you would want to do that, but some people enjoy being the "bad guy" at work. If you insist on being the bad guy and intentionally trying to create stress and pressure in the office, don't act surprised when you have some backlash. And get ready for a few "I told you so's"!

The key here is to try to run your business and your life with respect for the leadership role that you fill. Just as doctors are constantly acting on behalf of their entire profession, remember that you are acting on behalf of your reputation.

Always evaluate your decisions by the effect they will have on others. You need to control the quality of your reputation, so make decisions that will enhance those qualities you value. Don't sacrifice long-term relationships for short-term benefits. If you have to make a decision that will affect people in a negative way, do so in a manner that is dignified and allows everyone to continue on with their honor. In the end, your reputation, decisions, and actions will have the biggest impact on building positive momentum for your business.

And with any luck, your employees will come to respect you again.

2

Why doesn't anything ever get done on time?

Because Your Management Team Is Incompetent.

Don't have any managers? Then it falls on you, why aren't you managing your team?

There are dozens of respected theories on management. Beyond that, every manager I've ever talked to has a personal variation of management that seems to fit in with his or her own style. Most of these styles center on how the manager interacts with the employees he or she supervises.

What these managers tend to forget is that their primary responsibility is making sure things get done, they get done on time, and they get done right the first time. Imagine if you were to base your next performance review of your management team solely on those three criteria. How well would your managers score? How well would you score?

It takes quite a bit of skill to get a group of individuals to come together and work as a team, so I have a lot of respect for good managers. The best managers understand their priorities. They put the company first, making sure the company is reaching its goals. They are willing to sacrifice their time, their ego, and sometimes even their dignity in order to reach their goals. A great manager can do all of this and still earn the respect of the employees he or she supervises.

But most people that end up in management positions are complete failures. They get seduced by the power and authority they wield. Instead of focusing on the goals of the company, they focus on their own priorities. I call this phenomenon "empire building." It's the process of a manager trying to gather more and more authority, eventually creating a position of power that challenges even the owners of a company.

I've consulted with owners that were afraid to make changes to their business because it might upset one of their managers. This person had worked himself up so that he was essentially running the entire show—badly. When the owners wanted information, they were ignored. When they wanted to make changes, they were told it wasn't possible. When I came in, I fired his ass.

Empire builders are only in it for themselves and could care less about the business, the employees, or the customers. They don't belong in management, and they need to be rooted out as quickly as possible.

Then there are a few in management who are just unqualified for the position. This generally happens when they get promoted to head up the position they excelled at. For example, you could have a customer service superstar on your hands so you decide to promote her to customer service manager. It makes sense, you hope she will be able to show everyone else on the team how to become a superstar, too. Unfortunately, the skills to be a superstar in customer service are completely different from the skills needed to be a great manager.

The team is weaker because the strongest member is no longer doing what she does best, and your management team is weaker because you have someone in a position of power who doesn't have the skills or training to succeed. It's a lose–lose, and your company suffers.

The first step in getting more productivity from your employees is getting better managers. You have two choices on this: train the ones you've got, or go out and find new ones. Generally speaking, if you have bad managers now, no amount of training will make them better. They certainly could learn more about management, motivation, and productivity. But the problem is that they have lost the respect of the people they are supposed to manage. Once that is gone, you have to replace either the manager or the team. Guess which is easier. So my recommendation is to develop the right training for your managers, get new ones, and put them through the training. But don't ignore the fact that if your employees aren't getting their work done, it is a lack of motivation from management that is your problem.

Happiness isn't a requirement to have a highly motivated group. I'm sure when the pyramids in Egypt were being built, the workers were highly motivated. They accomplished some very impressive feats that are still around thousands of years later. But what was motivating the workforce, aspiring to do something great for humankind or the whip? I'd like to think we don't use that style of management anymore (although I have worked for some people who would like to bring it back!).

It wasn't all that long ago that the management debate was about which was more effective, the carrot or the stick. And even though there are still a lot of managers out there that would prefer to use the stick as a motivational tool, the workforce as a whole has rejected that method. A demanding, authoritative style may provide short-term performance, but it will never generate a genuine long-term commitment from your staff. A system that is fair and provides encouragement will always be more sustainable. It doesn't mean there shouldn't be consequences, but the focus on the motivation should be on encouragement, not punishment. The key question to ask yourself is this: are you inspiring your team by what they could accomplish or reminding your team of the consequences of failure?

To get the most out of your employees, motivational theories are everywhere, but there are two that I pay very close attention to. Understanding these theories can help you develop a strong sense of your team and create the type of culture in your business that will lead to long-term success.

The first theory comes from a psychologist name Frederick Herzberg, and it is called the Two Factor Theory. According to Herzberg there are two types of factors in the workplace. The first type of factors is linked directly to creating job satisfaction. The second type describes those factors that prevent job dissatisfaction.

It is the second set of factors that makes this theory so important. The table below shows a list of the factors in each type. As you can see, the type-two factors could be identified as more environmental while the type-one factors are more job related.

Type 1: Leading to Satisfaction	Type 2: Preventing Dissatisfaction
Achievement	Company Policy
Recognition	Supervision
Work Itself	Relationship with Boss
Responsibility	Work Conditions
Advancement	Salary
Growth	Relationship with Peers
	Security

So let's expand on this theory. You want to create better performance for your business, and in order to do that you need employees that are motivated to perform at a high level. According to Herzberg, in order to improve the satisfaction of your employees, you need to improve the characteristics listed in column one. Create a work environment that features those aspects, and you will see highly motivated individuals.

The items in column two are not motivational to employees. According to Herzberg, developing a better relationship with your boss will not improve your motivation. However, having a poor relationship with your boss will certainly cause dissatisfaction. The best way to think about column two is that these aspects are the minimum your business must supply in order to get people to work. Without these, your employees will become unhappy and leave.

It's interesting to look at because there are some big misconceptions out there about the types of things that are motivating to employees. If you look at column two, you'll see things like salary, peers, work conditions, and security. All of these things are thought of as motivating factors in most management circles. I've talked with business owners who have told me flat out they overpay their staff to make sure they stay motivated. What they are really doing is preventing these employees from becoming unhappy. But there is no increase in motivation.

For growth in your business, make sure you are meeting or exceeding the needs of your employees in column two. Then focus heavily on the items in column one. Increasing those benefits will launch your employees into a motivation frenzy!

The second motivational theory that I find very interesting is called the Expectancy Theory, which was developed by Victor Vroom. The fact that people perform actions to satisfy needs or wants is not anything groundbreaking. What Vroom noticed, though, is that not every person was motivated by the same types of desires. We can see this in almost any office. Not everyone is working as hard as they can each and every day even though the promise of a potential raise exists for all of them.

Vroom's answer to this is that tasks that are assigned at work are often the means to an end. Each individual is going to have secondary goals that have nothing to do with the goals of the organization. In Vroom's model a person is motivated by the potential reward and by the expectation that it can be achieved.

So back to our office example, it is possible that many of the staff members don't believe a raise is possible. Therefore, they won't try for it. Or it's possible that the staff could believe that a raise is inevitable whether they work hard or not. In that case, there wouldn't be any motivation to work harder. According to Vroom:

> This theory emphasizes the needs for organizations to relate rewards directly to performance and to ensure that the rewards provided are those rewards deserved and wanted by the recipients.[1]

Herzog and Vroom agree that motivation really needs to come from the employee. As the employer, your job is to create goals and structure where it is very clear that rewards are directly linked to performance. In other words, it is up to you and your management team to create the environment that promotes performance. So get managers who are skilled at personal relationships and understand that each individual is motivated by different things. Managers who know how to get the most out of their people are more valuable to you than managers who know how to perform the tasks of the people they supervise. Remember that, and you will always have a productive team.

1–Patrick J. Montana and Bruce H. Charnov, *Management*, 4th ed. (Barron's Educational Series, Inc., 2008).

3

Why does it feel like my company never gains any momentum?

Because You Don't Pay Attention To The Consequences Of Your Actions.

So we all know these words: "For every action there is an equal reaction." But what you might not know is that momentum is the sum of all the reactions your business creates.

On a recent trip to the coast, I was standing on the beach with my son trying to build a sand castle. As we were building, the waves kept creeping up closer and closer. Eventually, as the tide came in, the sand castle was wiped out. It took three good-sized waves to knock down the wall we had built up. After that, it only took two waves to wipe out the rest of the sand castle. It was my son's first experience trying to build a sand castle on the beach, so it was fun to watch him try to save his masterpiece even as the waves were washing it away.

Yes, the link to momentum is obvious. No, I'm not going to insult you by pointing it out. It's what I saw in the waves that really made an impression on me. Most of the time, the waves crashed at about the same spot. Those waves reached about the same height on the beach, and they retreated at about the same pace. But every once in a while, you'd get a big wave.

You could see that big wave coming. It broke a little higher up on the beach, and it rolled a little farther. But there wasn't any strength to it. When those waves came, they might reach the sand castle, but they wouldn't overcome it. They flowed right around the wall. Then they receded back to the ocean.

It was an amazing sight as they went back. These larger waves actually retreated with enough force to create a back wave, which would crash into the other waves coming in and create a very cool vertical spray. They also held back other waves. After one of these waves came through, my son had plenty of time to work on his sand castle before another wave threatened it.

The waves that crushed my son's sand castle were the ones we called piggyback waves. One wave would crash and slowly roll up the beach. While it was still coming, a second wave would ride on top of it. That second wave had the advantage of not touching the sand so it moved farther up the beach and faster. Those waves were devastating to the walls and eventually the castle.

Just like the waves, your business is affected by momentum through every action it takes. Every action can build positive or negative momentum. Businesses that are struggling and losing ground are building negative momentum. Desperation sets in, and more bad decisions are made. Nothing seems to work, and failure becomes a part of the culture. Expectations fall. The energy of the business disappears. The business is in real trouble.

Businesses that are growing and successful have positive momentum behind them. They are using the piggyback method to pair up positive actions to get better benefits. Customers are raving fans of the business. Revenue growth is breaking records. Happiness and excitement fill the offices. Employees believe everything they try will work out.

But most businesses fit somewhere in between. For every positive step forward, there is a negative set back. The momentum of the business keeps getting batted back and forth like the waves on the beach. For every big gain, there is a back wave that stops other successes from coming in. Rather than holding course, the strategy shifts continually with these businesses as they try to find some way to break through. Some businesses start chasing that one big deal, thinking it will solve everything.

These business owners are looking for the quick fix. Someone at the company usually starts the idea off with one really big prospect. "If we could just get this one deal, all of the other deals will be easier." More often than not, trying to get the "one big deal" will keep you from ever building consistent positive momentum. Even if you get the deal, the size of it will affect how you are able to service your existing customers. It can hold back future orders as you try to accommodate what you already have. If you fail to get the deal, you've invested time, money, and emotions into something that didn't deliver. Negativity grows. The back wave is building.

Before we can start working on building up momentum in your business, we need to identify where your business currently sits. Many times, businesses will have positive momentum in one area while suffering from negative momentum in others. For example, a business may be getting excellent reviews on its customer service, but product sales are down. Employee morale is high, but productivity is down. Are these businesses on the positive or negative side of momentum? Are they somewhere in the middle?

Having positive momentum lifts every part of your company. Just like the waves on a beach, if you don't pay attention to your momentum, your business will stall. You'll have a few good things happen; then a few bad things will come up, and you end up with a business that isn't failing but never gets the traction it needs to grow. It's normal for businesses to have periods of great success followed by periods of down time. Whether it's the seasonal nature of the business or the effects of the economy, no one can be on a continual upswing. What we want to do is build a consistent set of steps that keeps your business moving forward so that when the occasional down time hits, it doesn't become a trend.

To identify your current momentum, you need to take a whole view of your company. Be completely honest when you make your assessment. Negative momentum can be fixed, but only if you are willing to accept that it exists. Denial might be the one form of negativity that can't be overcome.

Businesses that have a strong positive momentum all share common traits. Having strong sales growth year after year is a major indicator that you are riding a wave of positive momentum. Sales growth is not the same as net income. There are a lot of factors that go into net income, and many of them are simply how expenses or revenue items are classified. When we are looking at momentum, net income is not one of the major factors we will be concerned with.

But look at your sales growth. Are you selling more than a year ago? If so, that's great and a definite sign that things are going well for you. If not, why not? Your sales numbers are an important indicator of whether or not your company is satisfying an ongoing need for your customers.

Pay attention to discounts and sales. Growth isn't just about the number of products that go out the door. Anyone can have a half-off sale and increase their product turnover. You want to focus on the dollars that are coming into the company. So the first step in identifying your momentum is to look at your sales numbers for the past few years and see just how well you are growing.

After you have a good idea of how the revenue is coming in to your business, start looking at your customers. If you have a strong positive momentum supporting your business, then you will have more than just customers—you will have fans. You will have people who are shouting from rooftops about your products and your service. They are telling everyone they know how great you are.

When was the last time your business got an unsolicited testimonial from a customer? Was it specific and heartfelt, or did it look like a form letter? A satisfied customer isn't good enough to be considered strong positive momentum. Satisfied means you met their minimum expectations. Satisfied means you did what you said you would do. Satisfied means the customer isn't going to complain. Satisfied is never going to be good enough. Get a good idea about what your clients and customers think about you, your business, your services, and your products.

Which brings us to the next function of your business—your products. How often are you introducing new products, solutions, and services to your market? When you have a steady stream of positive momentum, new products and new sales streams will develop automatically. Of course, the number of products you have will vary by industry. But in a growing business, your customers will be looking for new and exciting ways to buy from you. Are you providing them with what they want?

There are several other areas to look at when dealing with your products. How quickly are you able to bring a new product to market? With a lot of positive momentum behind you, your business should be able to meet or even anticipate the changing demands of the market. There are always opportunities in each market to solve additional problems with new products and services. Think of the graphic design company that also offers Web design and online marketing services. At first these may not have seemed to go together, but they fill a similar role and solve a similar problem in the marketplace. Look at how well you are satisfying all the needs of your target market.

Finally, take a look at your position in the market. Are you considered a market or industry leader? With the help of momentum, you can get free publicity for your company through interviews and publications. When you have a strong presence in your market, people are coming to you. You stop chasing down prospects and marketing opportunities. The market looks to you for guidance and respects you as a leader.

Not every business is going to have all these characteristics. But it's not a fantasy world either. Think about some of the major market leaders out there: Apple, Google, Amazon, etc. There are smaller companies that have similar success in their local markets. It isn't impossible to get to that point. Like I said earlier, you have to be willing to recognize where you are with your current momentum in order to get started on this path.

As a business owner, by nature you have a positive outlook on your business. You have problems, but hey, who doesn't? Things are going fine; you are just going through a rough spot right now. It's hard to look objectively at your performance. You still see the business as it should be, through the eyes of a visionary.

In order to grow, and by extension to reach that vision, you have to come to terms with where your company really is. It may be hard to hear, but very few businesses are riding high on the waves of positive momentum. Most businesses are struggling with momentum, taking two steps forward and then a step backward. That step backward is negative momentum building. If you let it continue, your business could end up on the wrong side of the momentum pendulum.

Momentum is powerful. It is the tipping point between business success and business failure. It grows from the cascading effects of your decisions and your actions. But what does momentum feel like? How do you know if momentum is working for you or against you?

If you have ever worked out at a gym or with weights of any kind, you know that momentum can play a big role. I've worked with several trainers in my time, and the one consistent message I hear is to have slow, controlled motions. There are several reasons for this.

First of all quick, jerky motions stress muscles too much. Taking a muscle from one movement to another quickly and with weight or resistance is a quick way to injury. It is also bad form for muscle development. The strength-building benefit of weights is lost when you don't respect the natural motion of the muscle.

Second, you need to use the appropriate amount of weight to get the biggest benefit. Too much weight and your form falls apart. You get no benefit and risk injury to other parts of the body. Too little weight and you get moving too fast, and the muscle never builds up.

Finally, momentum can carry you forward in your workout if you go too fast or inconsistently. Allowing your arms to extend fully or to jut out on exercises means you get the pendulum effect for the weight. It makes the load lighter on the way up. You use other parts of the body or other muscles to make a combined effort to get the weight up. If you aren't careful, you can not only hurt yourself, but you will fail to build any long-term growth in your exercise routine. The real momentum you are trying to build at the gym is long-term fitness.

At my gym, it's common to hear the trainers yell "Don't quit!" just as often as "Slow down." These professionals know that it takes sustained action in order to build up muscle mass and improve the fitness levels of their members. They also know that form and technique are more important than speed and power. Trying to be the fastest or the strongest at the gym is the fastest way to get injured. To build lasting improvement, go slow and never quit.

So let's apply this strategy or analogy to your business. How often is your business caught in fits and starts without any real movement? How often are you stuck in processes that never build on each other? How often do your internal teams have to work together to get a task done?

In a gym, momentum is based on mini successes and long-term growth. The focus is to build strength in the body. We don't want the momentum of swinging our arms to help us get through a single exercise. We want the long-term benefits of using proper form and technique to build the muscle and grow. In your business are you trying to build momentum in a short-term or long-term strategy? How often should you be yelling "Don't quit" and "Slow down" in your office?

Negative momentum is a wakeup call, not a death sentence for your business. Get yourself in the right mindset. It's actually a good thing if you can identify negative momentum in your business. It means you have a great understanding of where your business is and what needs to change to get back on the explosive growth path. So, what does it look like when you are suffering from negative momentum?

If positive momentum is all about sales growth, then negative momentum is going to be about a lack of sales growth. And I'm not just talking about falling sales. Even businesses that are barely growing or businesses that grow well in one quarter but lose in another quarter are fighting against some negative momentum.

Look at the trends of your sales and total income. Depending on your industry, you could see wide swings in sales from quarter to quarter. Compare your sales over several years if you can. If you were going to graph those numbers, which way would the line go—up, down, zigzag, or horizontal? What does that tell you about the momentum your business is carrying?

Along with sales, negative momentum will affect your products. Look at your inventory levels. Are they rising substantially? Do your products feel dated? Are you always trying to catch up to the competition? When momentum is working against you, it becomes more difficult to get creative. Clearance sales and other discounts become the norm in order to sell your product or service.

Instead of finding new ways to offer solutions in the market, you are spending all of your time chasing down new customers. This is where that mentality of finding that one big sale comes in. You are hoping for one contract or one sale that will stop the backslide and get you moving forward again. High inventory levels, a lack of repeat purchases from customers, and constant discounts are signs that your products aren't up to the expectations of the market.

Take a good look at the culture inside your business. What types of calls are your customer service people getting? Pay attention to their attitudes. As the complaints and returns build up, their morale and energy levels will start to drop. The first sign that morale is dropping will be rumors about layoffs or unexpected terminations.

Look at your management staff. Are they focused on growing the business or cutting costs? Most managers have been trained to work from their budget and make a difference through process and efficiency. They want a pat on the back for being able to cut costs and staying within budget. But while they are focused on the costs of the business, the customer is ignored. Managers also tend to cut some of the benefits that employees enjoy a little more often than they should. This is another sign employees take as a warning that the company is in trouble. Fear starts to be the only motivating factor in the office. See how the negativity grows?

Companies that are struggling with their momentum also have an unusually high turnover rate. As the fear builds, the rumors are proven true, the benefits get cut, and employees leave. They want something that feels more stable. Are your top employees starting to get lower performance ratings on their reviews? It can be a sign they aren't as invested in your company or their own success. It's a big indicator that things are not going well at your company. It is also a big push on momentum. As you lose your important employees, it becomes harder and harder to build that positive momentum you need to get back on the right track.

When faced with a hard decision, people tend to fall back on what they are most comfortable doing. If the problem you are facing isn't urgent, if there isn't an imminent danger or potential for failure, it's hard to get the motivation to change what you are doing. The business owner who only has enough cash to keep the doors open for another six months has a different motivation than the business owner who is flush with cash and just looking for ways to grow into a different industry.

But the paradox is, the desperate owner is more likely to fail even though he is more highly motivated. Why? He waited too long. When you get into that desperate state, the actions you take aren't about building momentum. They aren't about long-term success. The actions are about immediate survival.

Businesses that have solid sales but no growth are in a better position than companies that are shrinking by ten percent each year. You need to recognize that momentum is turning and keeping you from the success you want before it has taken over your company. Changing momentum is hard enough on its own. Don't make it harder by waiting until the last minute to try and fix everything.

For now I want you to classify your business as one of the following categories:

Positive Momentum: Things are going very well. Sales growth is consistent each year, and we are developing new solutions, products, and services for our customers. We are seen as a market innovator and a market leader. We consider our customers as part of our sales force because of the strong and supportive comments we receive from them.

Mixed Momentum: The business is strong, but we have things to work on. Our sales growth has been inconsistent year after year. Sometimes we see growth; other times we have fallen back. We understand the market but haven't become a major player just yet. Our customers are great, and our products are good quality, but we have the same issues all companies deal with. We occasionally go through bouts of morale issues and have some turnover. If we could get one more big client, it would really help us turn the corner.

Negative Momentum: Sales are down. Stress and tension are very visible inside the organization. We are getting complaints from our customers, and new products are not being developed. Right now our major focus is on cutting costs to survive this current down turn in revenue. Our sales team is focused on bringing in a major account to help us get back on our feet.

Now there are certainly shades of gray between each of these three categories, but my experience tells me most companies fit in to the mixed momentum category. The good news is that the sweet spot for making a change falls very close to that section.

When we talk about the excitement of a business, or its "wow factor," we are really talking about momentum. Is the business growing or dying? Do people love it, tolerate it, or hate it? Momentum can be the great multiplier of your success and growth, or it can work against you when you are in a slow and comfortable pace. Ever try to go out and run a 10K race? I've seen people go from the couch to the race without any training. Wanna guess how well they did? Their momentum was all about the couch work. Now look at the person who trains for weeks leading up to the race. She gets a mile run, then a 5K, and then on race day she is ready to finish the race successfully.

Whether you decide to take action or not, momentum is going to respond. Don't let inaction or inattentiveness run your company. A strong respect for the power of momentum can change your outlook on your business. It can give you the push you need to make the changes necessary to keep momentum working for you. Think of momentum as your business partner. Do you want a partner that builds your business or one that brings it down?

Look at you business, your relationships, your health, and your life in the same way. To find success, you really have to build up your momentum in every part of your life. You can't take your business or career from nothing to greatness overnight. It won't happen waiting on the sidelines either. You have to actively want it. You have to actively work for it.

4

Why are we losing customers?

Because They Don't Like Your Company.

There was a sandwich shop just a couple of blocks from my house. They made the most amazing turkey sandwich ever. The bread was perfect; it had a good crust and was sturdy enough to handle all the toppings. The sandwich was loaded with veggies and enough oil and vinegar that if you let it sit too long, your hands were going to get messy. Even if you pinched this thing down, you couldn't get your mouth around it in one bite. In short, I loved this place.

One day I walked in to get my sandwich, and the prices had jumped over a dollar per sandwich. I still placed my order, and as I was waiting I got to hear about the hardships of the shop. Food costs went up and they tried to ride it out but couldn't, and so they had to pass some of the cost on to their customers. I appreciated them telling me the story; it was reasonable, and I left without thinking too much more about it.

A week or so later, I went back for my sandwich and found a little note hanging on the cash register saying "Due to rising food costs, we are raising prices on all our items. Sorry." A little cold, but I imagine after a week or so of telling everyone what happened, you get tired of the complaints. Maybe this was a little easier.

It took several weeks before I made it back in. Now there were several signs inside the shop. The prices had gone up again. My sandwich was smaller and certainly not stuffed as full as normal. I left quietly, wondering if this was just an off day or if the sandwiches really had changed. The following week, I went to another sandwich shop. I was talking to the owner, and the conversation went to food costs. He said there was a little bump in pricing a couple months ago but nothing too big. I walked out wondering why my favorite sandwich shop was trying to drive me away.

Maybe they did have an increase in their food costs, and maybe they were stuffing way more food into those sandwiches than what they could afford based on their prices. But why were they being so public about it? Did they think we as customers were going to find a way to lower their costs? Did they think we wouldn't shop around and see if other sandwich places were raising their prices? It kept going around in my head, and I just couldn't shake the feeling that this company didn't understand how they were treating their customers.

Over time, I stopped going completely. After every visit I had buyer's remorse. The product wasn't as good, the service wasn't as friendly, and I felt a little cheated by the company. In other words, I didn't like the company anymore. It sold soon after, and then sold again. I tried it one other time, but it wasn't any better. It just stopped being the kind of company I wanted to give my money to.

So what kind of company are you? It's easy to make decisions about the direction of your company from a conference room with an income statement in your hand. Cut here, raise prices here, stop these services, give less there. But do you ever step back and think how these decisions will change your company?

The next time you want a cup of coffee, skip your favorite franchise and drive past the parking lot coffee stand. Find yourself a breakfast diner and take a seat at the counter. Leave your electronic devices in the car, and grab a newspaper on the way in. Relax for just a minute, read your paper, and drink your coffee. Then take a moment to size up the waiter or waitress who has been serving you coffee. Did he have a smile? Ask you questions? Leave you alone? Did she seem friendly? When you walk out of the diner, think about your overall experience. Why was this different than your normal cup of coffee?

The answer has to do with the difference between customer service and customer loyalty. When you get your marketing figured out and you start building some momentum, you should have customers lining up around the corner to work with you. Money starts flying in the door, and all that stress and pressure that you were feeling starts to melt away. You begin sleeping at night again. Well, wake up, Bubba, because your job ain't done yet.

Developing the right culture is the only way you can create the type of company customers love being around and spending their money with. The best experience I had with a company's culture was when I worked for a very large catalog retail company. The career life for a call center agent is very short, but I was one of the exceptions to that rule. I was hired just before the holiday season rush, and I got very little training. It was sink or swim for those of us who got hired in that last round of interviews.

The training I did get, however, was amazing. Under normal conditions, new hires would get two full weeks of training before interacting with customers. I was one of the last to be hired for that year. It was coming up on Thanksgiving, and I was told right away that my training would be cut down to a week.

That year we had one of the worst winter storms ever for our area. It shut down the city for two days. People were without heat and electricity. You literally could not drive on most of the roads. And my training was cut from five to three days.

I wasn't alone. The company would hire call center agents in groups of ten to twenty. So there were a lot of us who knew we weren't getting the training we needed. Our spirits were down because we already knew our time was short with the company. High-volume retail companies hire for the holiday season, and then lay off the excess in January. Being the last group hired—and the least trained—meant we were on the fast track to the layoff line.

But here is where this company made a brilliant move. More specifically, here is where our training director made a brilliant move. The company was built on a reputation for outstanding customer service. The phone agents were well-known to help customers by going way beyond the call of duty. Our training director decided to scrap the training program completely and start something brand new right there on the fly.

Instead of training our group about the products in the catalog so we could answer questions, our training director told us about how each product is available for us to view. She told us stories of agents who would put customers on hold, run over to the product area, and grab the product to describe in detail all of the features and benefits of the dress or sweater or knickknack. She went to the marketing department, grabbed two years' worth of old catalogs, and gave them to us so that we could have reference materials in case there were questions.

Then instead of teaching us the software program, which required a minimum of four days, she showed us how to place a simple order in the system and then taught us how to write everything else down on paper order forms. When we groaned a little, she started telling us stories about how even though the training was canceled because of the recent bad weather, customer service had not. Agents had made their way into the call center to take calls and write down the orders for people. With the computer systems down, these agents made commitments to call each one of these customers back once the order was entered into the system. If they could do it under those circumstances, surely we could do it, too.

On the third and final day of training, we were very nervous about going out and starting. Our trainer knew it and made sure we understood the company's expectation of us. She told us that nothing was more important than helping the customer. The company understood that 80 percent of its revenue came from 20 percent of its customer base. It identified these top customers and automatically enrolled them in a VIP program. She told us that while all of our customers were important, we needed to pay special attention to these particular customers. A compliment from one of them went a long way with the company and a complaint could ruin our chances at staying.

Toward the end of that last day, she told us the story of how she became the head of the training department. A few years prior, she was a call center agent just like we were. She was working on Christmas Eve and took a call from one of these VIP customers. This customer was in a panic. She had placed some orders with our company as gifts for her family, and they had arrived on time. But the gifts she had ordered from another company hadn't arrived yet, and when she called that company she was told the items were on backorder and wouldn't be shipped until January.

She was in tears. Her family was coming in from different parts of the country, and half of the gifts she needed weren't going to be there. "I know it's last minute, but is there anything you can do for me?"

It was Christmas Eve. Even with an overnight delivery, no one delivered on Christmas day. It would have been easy for our trainer to have said, "I'm really sorry, but there's nothing I can do." Heck, most people would even throw in a little "Next time you'll know to just order from us!" But that wasn't the expectation at this company. Customer service first and foremost. So instead of dismissing this, our trainer stepped up and said, "Let's see what we can do."

For forty-five minutes the two of them went through the catalog and found items to fill her gift list that were all in stock. The trainer physically went to the warehouse, pulled every one of the items, took them back to her desk, and called this lady back to let her know she had the items in her hands and was going to do whatever she could to make sure they were delivered.

She called delivery companies and couldn't find anyone that would make the delivery. By now most of the call center had heard what was going on, and instead of snickering or making fun of what she was trying to do, they pitched in. Between calls they got wrapping paper and started wrapping each of the presents. As it got later in the day, no one knew for sure how to get the gifts to this customer.

Our trainer called her again, prepared to give her the bad news. When the customer answered the phone, she decided that she had simply gone too far already and couldn't disappoint her customer. Instead of saying, "I'm sorry, I did all I could, but I can't get these gifts to you," she said, "Mary, I need directions to your house. I'm on my way with your gifts."

She drove five hours that afternoon to personally deliver an order to a customer. She ended up having to stay the night in a hotel and came back home on Christmas day. When she returned to work, the CEO of the company was waiting at her desk with a huge smile and gave her a hug. He immediately put her in charge of training.

That story became part of the company's history and part of the customer experience mystique. Agents tried at different levels to match or best the story, but it always lived on as the perfect example of going the distance for your customers.

As for me and my group of untrained rejects, all but one of us kept our jobs through the layoff period. It was a huge change in the training program at that time. The focus of training had always been on the how, with a little sprinkling of the why. Our class got all of the why and none of the how. We made it work because we knew how important it was to the culture of the company. And it is amazing how well people will perform when they have that perfect vision of what they are supposed to aspire to.

I was with that company long enough to see it grow too big. This story and many others like it lost their place in the culture of the company. As it grew, things like this were no longer "feasible" and they didn't make "economical sense." Customer service was still important, but it was no longer the focus. Process improvement, inventory reduction, upselling, and cost cutting became the major focus of the company in later years. While the company became more profitable with this new focus, its best growth years were when it was focused on the customer.

I always wonder, though, how big and amazing would that company have been if it remained true to its history and remembered that its customers are the most important part of its business.

If you are going to keep growing your customer base, you better have a dynamic customer experience. You can have the perfect marketing plan, but if customers show up and are disappointed by what they see, you will never get their money. Even if you do get their money once, did you do enough to earn a repeat visit? Did you earn a referral from them? What are they going to tell their best friends about you?

Today's customer experience is heavily influenced by technology. Before we can talk about how to build your customer experience, we need to talk about the Internet. It was 1994 when things really started to change for businesses. The Internet was gaining in popularity. Those with access to the Internet understood just how big of an opportunity this could be, but it didn't seem like anyone was capitalizing on it. But a small little company out in Seattle, Washington, decided to give this Internet thing a try.

Amazon has become a major retailer, doing massive business year after year, and has anyone ever walked into an Amazon store? Have you gone to a checkout counter and talked to a sales associate as she rang up the books and fleece jacket you just bought? Think about it, how does a company get this big without someone focused on one-to-one customer service? Amazon was the company that really changed what a customer expects from a retailer.

In the late 1990s, there were online retailers everywhere. Investors were looking for the next EBay or Amazon, and they were throwing money at any company that could prove it was getting traffic. Because the industry was so new, no one thought to ask if any of these companies was making money. Instead they just kept investing. Then the online world shifted, and business has never been the same.

Everything fell apart. These businesses had no income. No one was buying from anonymous Web sites. Businesses realized that the average consumer didn't trust Web sites inherently. They would trust brands they recognized, but to give personal information over the Internet was still too new. Consumers also didn't like waiting for their purchases to be delivered. Part of the psychology of spending is the reward of having your shiny new object in your hand immediately. In short, consumers still held on to the comfort of their past shopping experiences in a store, with real people and real products.

When the investment dollars were spent, these companies declared bankruptcy, closed up shop, and sent the economy into the toilet. So a few lessons were learned by business owners and investors, and the Internet world started to get a facelift.

This led to new innovations on the Web. Secure shopping carts were added to Web sites. Faster delivery speeds were added, and shipping costs were reduced. Return policies were upgraded to let consumers try products out and return them if they weren't satisfied. As consumer confidence grew, self-service became the new craze. Rather than waiting in line, you could now point, click, pay, and move on with your day. During the 2000s, businesses successfully changed consumer behavior to first trust, then to prefer an online experience.

That shift happened while we all were watching, but not too many of us were paying attention. It was like cleaning your house with the TV on. You could hear it, and you knew it was on, but you had no idea what just happened on the show because you were focused on something else. How many business owners understand what that shift really did to their customers?

The Internet has created an unprecedented number of choices for customers. More importantly, it has expanded the access customers have to new products. At any given time, a customer can purchase from one of your competitors. The Internet takes orders all day every day. There are no store hours for a Web site. It's always there, ready to show off products and take an order.

So to combat this increase in competition, you as a business owner put up your own Web site. If you were a retail company to start with, you probably hired sales associates to work in the store. These people greeted new customers, helped them find products, educated them on the quality of the products in your store, rang up the sales, and took care of these customers in general. But with a Web site, you now need people who can answer questions about the site. They are no longer there to help customers understand or upsell the products; they are there to handle problems and deal with returns and complaints. Welcome to the customer service shift.

Customer service has shifted from a "before the sale" activity to a "maintain the sale" role. As businesses train consumers that self-service is better, we are inadvertently training consumers that qualified sales associates are unnecessary. All these consumers really need is someone to tell them why their shipment hasn't arrived yet. This is the shift that is destroying the customer experience of so many businesses.

How do you define your customer-service program? If you are like most businesses, you will point to your customer-service department and talk about the different functions that each member or group performs. You will brag about how many great comments you get about the quality of your service. Your marketing might even go so far as to say you are number one in customer service (guess what, you aren't the only one that's number one).

Of course, all of that means you have completely missed the point on customer service. Think about it: If your customer service team is there to handle customer problems, complaints, and returns (like most customer-service teams), why is it so big? Have you ever heard a business owner talk about how everyone in the company is responsible for customer service? What does that tell you: "We have so many problems with our product or ordering process that it takes our entire staff to handle the complaints." Not exactly the message you want to be sending out. In fact, if you are staffing more people to handle your customer service than you are to handle your sales, then I would say you have a customer-service issue.

That wonderful service your employees provide may get you a few good testimonials, but in the long run it is going to hurt your overall momentum. Consumers have been trained that dealing with people is a hassle. If they have to deal with a person for any reason, they will associate negatively with your business—even if the service was first class. The more times they find themselves dealing with your customer-service team, the less likely they are to buy from you again.

What does it all mean? The Internet, ecommerce, and self-service have changed consumer attitudes toward retailers. Amazon figured this out early. It's not about the customer service anymore. They don't need a person dedicated to helping customers make a buying decision. They have created a customer experience that meets the needs of their consumers. You need to start thinking in terms of the customer experience and forget about being number one in customer service!

Let's go back to our cup of coffee at the diner. You have a choice every day about how you will take your coffee. You can home brew it. You can go to a franchise or a drive-up coffee stand. If you want, you can slow down and go to a diner. Every one of these choices provides you with a vastly different experience. There may be a slight difference in the quality of the coffee, but in general we buy based on the experience we expect to get.

If you want to relax, you might be more inclined to go to the diner and sit down for a few minutes. If you are in a hurry, you might choose a franchise or a coffee stand. The bottom line is that as a consumer, the experience we have is just as powerful in making a decision as the quality or price of the product. This is a powerful realization that many business owners tend to ignore.

It can be devastating to spend the time and do the work to generate true positive momentum in your business and then lose it because you forgot to pay attention to the customer. Your competition is no longer the business across town. You don't have the luxury of a "convenient location" or being "the only game in town" as a way to keep your customers. Consumers know they can use a simple mouse click and get your product or service from anywhere in the world. If you want to maintain your momentum and grow your business, you need to get your mind right about customer service.

Right here, right now, I want you to let go of your views of whatever you think customer service is. It is no longer the thing you do best. You are no longer number one at customer service. Stop thinking that your amazing customer-service team is what makes you better than your competition. And get your amazing customer service out of all your marketing materials. In the eyes and especially the pocketbooks of your customers, your customer service doesn't make a bit of difference. Replace it with your focus on the customer experience.

How are you controlling your customer's overall experience with your company? It starts with their first introduction to you and goes all the way to the delivery of your product or service. In companies that really understand the customer experience, it also includes the reorder and referral process. The important point to understand is that customer service is not the same as your customer experience. Customer service is only a part of the whole customer experience. As you start developing what your customer experience is going to be, you will be responsible for making sure every person in your company understands his or her role in that experience.

The reason so many companies fail to build a loyal customer following is because they don't make this very important distinction. There are five phases to your customer experience, and customer service is only one part of that. Let's put customer service in its place. Customer service is your problem-solving center. It is vital to your ongoing success, but only if it is done right. Think about your favorite theme park. What is more important to the customer—the rides, the attractions, the experience, or the person sitting in the information booth?

So ask yourself: What does it feel like to be a customer of my company? You know what you want it to be like, and you probably have some misconceptions about what it really is. You will have to find a way to ignore all of that. Get a realistic view of how your company treats its customers. The only way to do that is to meet some of your clients or customers face to face and have a genuine conversation with them.

Ask them questions about what motivated them to buy from you. Find out what their experiences were when they placed an order or followed up with your company. Ask them why they did or did not reorder from you. Don't just rely on your marketing team to get this information. As a business owner, when you spend the time with your customers firsthand, you get a direct view of what your company is really doing. You get the uncensored feedback about what your company does well and where you are letting your clients down. Don't skip this step, and don't delegate it!

I know of one business owner who would occasionally call in to purchase items from his staff to gauge firsthand what kind of experience was being delivered. His office normally closed at five each evening. As a test, he would call a few minutes before five and try to place a complicated order. Or he would ask to speak with various departments about a previous purchase. He wanted to make sure that the same service was being given to the last customer of the day as it was to the first. You can imagine the insight he was getting about the quality of his customer experience. He was able to incorporate changes in the way calls were handled and followed up on to give a better experience to his customers.

So as you are getting feedback about what you are currently providing as a customer experience, start making notes about what you really want that experience to look and feel like. Take suggestions from your long-time clients. Sometimes what you think is important doesn't matter as much to your customers. Again, think like you are building a theme park. You need to focus on all of the details—from the time your customer walks into your business all the way to the time he or she comes back again.

I have identified five phases that all of the best customer experiences embrace. In order to build an amazing experience for your customers, you will need to address each of these phases. Overall your customer experience needs to reflect the entire relationship your business will have with each customer. The first phase is the Introduction followed by Browsing, Purchasing, Service/Support, and finally Referral/Reorder. Notice how Purchasing is in the middle and not at the end? Businesses with a strong customer experience understand that the sale is not the end of your relationship with your customer.

The first phase of the customer experience is really going to be handled by your marketing team. This is the Introduction phase. Think of it as your first impression. When you show up to the office, are you wearing a suit or are you more casual? What about your other employees? Is there a dress code? Now think about the image of your business. Are your appearance and your business's image a match? What about the services and messaging you are offering? Do they match the image you are trying to portray with your business?

I've worked with professional sales offices that wanted to promote a relaxed atmosphere. They didn't want to show off the suits and ties. The company allowed khakis and polo shirts. But the décor in the office was ultramodern with high-end furniture and art. When customers walked in, they were confused about what they saw. The professionalism of many of the salespeople was questioned because they didn't dress like they belonged at that company. First impressions are a big deal when trying to build a customer experience.

The next part of the customer experience is the Browsing phase. At a clothing store, this would be when the shopper goes from rack to rack looking at different shirts, touching the fabric and checking the care instructions on the tag before going to the dressing room to try them on. In a restaurant, this would be where the diners sit down and take in the ambiance of the dining room. They look over the menu and try to find the meal choice that sounds the best.

For most businesses, however, this is really the Web site test. Consumers are looking around for any hint that you may not be all you seem. They are checking to see what your return policies are. They are looking for comments, referrals, and testimonials about your company. And they are looking at the quality of your products and services.

The Browsing phase is where you can make a huge impression on your customers. I'm going to stay with the theme-park analogy through this, so be prepared. When you are driving up to a theme park, you already have an emotional connection to your childhood. As you get closer, the tracks of the roller coaster come into view, and those emotions turn into anticipation. You think about your previous experiences and even tell stories to your kids about what it was like when you were their age. You are trying to create that kind of anticipation with your customer experience. And anticipation is a powerful motivator that puts consumers in a buying mood.

Be bold and creative as you create a browsing experience for your customers. Try and incorporate as many senses as you can with your experience. People may go to a movie theater thinking they are going to skip the popcorn, but one smell of that buttery goodness and we are all at the counter forking over half a paycheck for a tub. What you want your browsing experience to do is build the anticipation and drive your customers to the next phase.

After consumers are done browsing, they move straight to the Purchasing phase. In terms of thinking about the customer, this phase is regularly overlooked by businesses big and small. This is the moment when the consumer is ready, willing, and able to give you money—don't mess this up now!

I can remember many years ago, I was in a large department store looking for jeans. I had been wandering around the men's section for quite some time and hadn't found anything that I really liked. Fortunately, a sales associate came over and started talking with me. She showed me a couple of styles I hadn't looked at before, and we mixed and matched some new shirts as well. I went in expecting to buy one or maybe two pairs of jeans. I had four pairs of pants and three shirts in my hands, and I was ready to pay.

I had come out of the dressing room, and the sales associate was gone. I looked around for someone else and couldn't find any employees in that department. I wandered around the store looking for anyone to help me, and I couldn't find a single store employee. I went back to the men's department and waited a few minutes. I finally saw an employee, but she completely ignored me and walked on to another department. Frustrated, I could have walked out of the store and not purchased anything. But I'm a little more unconventional than that.

Instead of throwing down the clothes and walking out, I jumped up on the checkout counter and took a seat. I waved to everyone I saw. Within minutes I had two salespeople walking quickly to that counter ready to help me. I handed them all of the clothes I picked out and told them I only wanted the two pairs of jeans I had come in for. I got my jeans, but they lost out on over half of the money I was willing to spend because no one was there to help me. It was the last time I shopped in that store.

Bottom line, you need to make it easy for your customers to spend their money with you. Don't add unnecessary steps. Have you been to a store lately that asks for your phone number or your zip code before they will take your money? If I'm just there for a small purchase, something like that can make me think twice about coming back. Why would I want to answer a questionnaire before I buy a pack of gum? Remember, make it easy. Don't give your customers any reason to doubt their choice to spend money with you.

Look at your Web site. Is it easy to check out? Don't think people are willing to do more work just to order online. Make it simple and fast. Also, train your employees to take an order over the phone or in person. Don't let a policy or a lack of training stop a customer who is ready to give you his money. More sales are lost because the business made it too difficult or confusing to complete the sale than at any other point in the process.

We have finally reached the Support phase of the customer experience, and this is where your customer-service team will fit in. If everything you did was perfect, you would never have a need for this phase. But we don't live in a world of perfect, so there needs to be a way for you to support your customers after the sale. Remember, this is your problem-solving team. If this team is getting big and is always too busy, there is a problem somewhere else in the company.

Build this experience so that it is easy for your customers to get the answers they are looking for. Remember, when customers contact you after the sale, they aren't looking for excuses or reasons why something bad happened. They want solutions. They want answers. How you handle this experience for your customers will determine your long term reputation in the market.

The biggest key to creating a successful support experience is accessibility. Make sure that your customers and clients have multiple ways to contact your company and request help. Even though self-service is the trend, don't rely on simple e-mail contact forms and a frequently-asked-questions Web page to handle your customer service. Offer instant chat options. Make it easy for your customers to get a live person on the phone. The quicker you get a solution in front of your customers, the better.

When you have a team that is responsible for dealing one-on-one with your clients, you need to empower them to resolve issues right then and there. Nothing frustrates customers and ruins the experience quicker than talking to someone who can't fix your problem. Think about the overall experience. If your customer spends fifteen minutes explaining a problem to your customer-service team and then has to be transferred somewhere else, there is going to be some frustration building up. If after that transfer, the customer needs to talk to yet another person, you have lost this customer forever.

I have seen customer service offered both ways. I worked for a company that allowed the customer-service team to resolve issues immediately, without the need to check in with a supervisor. The customer-service team was coached consistently on how to resolve conflict and get the customer to a solution without allowing anything to escalate. This company became very well-known for their customer service. Most of the other companies I've dealt with allow very minimal decision making by their front-line staff. The majority of decisions have to be cleared by a supervisor or manager. This method may feel safer for the company, but it tends to lead customers and your staff down a path of frustration. If you are strong enough, I highly recommend you empower your employees to resolve issues on the spot without needing a manager to approve anything.

Depending on your particular business model, you are going to have to make decisions about how you build out the customer experience in the Support phase. Customers who have already made one purchase with you are much more likely to buy again if they have a great experience. Each of these steps is leading up to the Reorder phase where you are getting new orders from existing customers. Don't let your customer-service team ruin your momentum by creating a stressful or difficult customer experience.

In the Reorder phase, your entire company is working to remind your customers of the amazing experience they had with you. This is the loyalty test. How many of your customers moved past "satisfied" and have become fans? Are you getting referrals? How many testimonials are you getting? Are your existing clients or customers purchasing other products from you?

To help get the answers you are looking for, think about how easy it is for your clients to reorder from you. Find a way to build new anticipation, either with new products or with added perks for working with your company. This is the phase where you start thinking about incentive or rewards programs.

There are a lot of incentive or rewards programs out there. Most of them are centered on discounts or special offers at periodic times of the year. But these programs are so generic that they never have a chance at building customer loyalty.

Make sure you have created a process to segment out your best clients. You can measure your clients' behavior in many ways—number of orders, size of orders, total revenue, market influence, etc. The point is, make sure you have a method to differentiate the customers who have the biggest impact on your bottom line. These are the clients you want to focus on with any type of incentive program. They are also the clients who will give you the most valuable information about how to build and improve your customer experience.

Let me leave you with an example of one company that knew how to maximize the customer experience.

I enjoy sending flowers and other small gifts to those people who are close to me. After a couple of orders with one florist, I was contacted directly and asked if I wanted to sign up for a frequent buyer program. I wasn't all that interested at first, but the company offered an online calendar for me where I could fill out reminders of special events. Not only that, but when the reminders came up, they would offer suggested gifts based on the events and what was currently in stock.

I don't know how hard that was for them to set up. But for me, it was perfect. I didn't have to try to remember these things on my own. I didn't have to go through a catalog and pick out the right gift. I was getting an e-mail that said, "Next week is your anniversary. Here are some suggested arrangements," and there were four or five pictures of some beautiful flowers. All I had to do was a couple of quick clicks, and I was able to move on with my day.

But think of it from their point of view. They got easy reorders from me. Not only that, they could control their inventory by tailoring the options sent to me. Because gifts and flowers can be seasonal, they could offer me choices based on the items they had in stock. It was an amazing focus on the customer experience.

If you are going to put together an incentive program, make sure it ties in to the overall customer experience, much like the florist did. I didn't get any discounts on those arrangements or for signing up to their program. What I got was an amazing service that made it easy for me to reorder. The focus of your program should be based on what will make your customers place another order with you.

Now, what are you going to do for your customers?

5

Why is our competition growing while we struggle to survive?

Because You Are Failing To Establish Yourself As A Market Leader.

Need to blow your nose? Go grab a Kleenex. Need to make a copy of a document? Xerox it. Need skates for your kids? Get some Rollerblades.

When your company name becomes synonymous with the product you sell, then you know you are leading the market. I mean, does anyone know who made the second copier? Brands that reach this level of recognition in the market are not struggling for sales. Do you really think Wal-Mart needs to worry about whether or not they are going to make their rent payment next month? Of course, massive recognition and a consistent flow of sales is not the same as profitability. So I guess these massive companies can still screw it all up.

They could be inefficient and waste money. They could stop worrying about quality and let their products turn to crap. They could offend their market with a really bad message or by doing something stupid like polluting a river. But the main way these companies can screw it up is by forgetting what they did to get on top the first time—by leading the market.

Being a leader is about more than just being first to release a product. Your company has to be able to adjust to new market influences and continue to put out the products and services your customer base is looking for.

Do you need to have this kind of market recognition to be recognized as a leader? No, but it sure helps.

Being a market leader is about more than having the most sales or being the biggest company. In fact, many of the largest companies in an industry are too big to be able to adjust quickly enough to lead a changing marketplace. Leading a market is about being the resource everyone looks to. For years Microsoft was the biggest company in the computing industry. But if you wanted to talk to someone about the future of computing devices, Apple would be at the top of that list now. That is the benefit of being the market leader. You become the person or the entity that everyone thinks of in your industry.

You can carve out a nice little niche for your business. Get a few routine customers who buy enough to pay your bills and then pick up a few new customers here and there to squeeze out a small profit. There are little shops everywhere that have decided to make that their business model. And who am I to say that is the wrong strategy? It works for them. At least until someone or something comes along that can produce it faster, cheaper, and more consistently. Then they are out of business. Ask anyone who lost their business when a national retailer moved in to their small community.

Running a small business is too often a balancing act between having enough to survive and spending enough to grow. Business owners are tied in to the community they serve and feel every bump and bruise that community goes through. Whether it's a small rural community or a major metropolitan area, when the community suffers, so do all the small businesses. With all that uncertainty, how can a small business owner feel confident about risking it all to grow the business? It's a simple matter of necessity. If you choose to keep your business small and allow yourself to think small, you will be subject to all the winds of change that blow through your community. But if you choose to think big, take big actions, and focus on leading your market, then you have a chance to rise above it all and bring long-term success to your business.

Let me tell you the story of two business owners, Danny and Ricky, who were competitors in the same industry and were each trying to be recognized as the leaders of their market. The owners of each company had tremendous knowledge of the industry. I did some work for both of these companies, and I was amazed at the difference in approach each business owner took toward their market. It would be easy to recognize each of them as experts in the field, but only Ricky found that success. Danny, while able to service his customers well, never reached the same level of recognition.

Ricky recognized early on that credibility was a major factor with potential customers. He spent quite a bit of time and money to get himself and his staff certified with many of the professional organizations in his industry. These certifications weren't nationally known, and were limited to the current industry. For example, these weren't project management or technology certifications. But the designations were important in his industry and made a difference to his customer base, so he made sure his company was well represented.

I have seen many decision makers hold back on industry certifications because they never put much significance to them. It is true that these certifications don't mean much in the wider business community, but that really isn't your market, is it? If a certification or training has meaning in your industry, then it should be important to your company.

Danny also understood the importance of credibility in his industry. But he saw the certifications as a complete waste of time and money. They didn't teach anything new, and his staff turned over enough that investing in certifying them would not be practical. He focused exclusively on promoting his experience and his expertise in the industry. In fact, he had more years in the industry than most of the people offering the certifications. His knowledge was unquestioned, and he knew he would be able to sell it to his prospects.

This is very common with business owners. You know your industry inside and out. Most likely you had years of experience with these products and services before you even opened your doors. You might even have an internal training program that seems to work well. But look at it from the point of view of your customers. How do they know you and your company are keeping up to date on the latest research in your market? How do they know you have the type of company that holds itself to a higher standard? On a more basic level, how are you going to find the time to keep yourself, your team, and your customers up to date on all the latest trends? You may not believe the certifications are worth the money or time to you, but they are very valuable to the success of your business.

In a heavily regulated industry, Ricky understood that if he wanted to be recognized as the leader, he needed to get involved with people who had influence over the regulations. He reached out in his network and found several advisory committees for his industry. With his background and certifications, he was welcomed to most of them and quickly gained influence in the industry. He soon started forming his own committees and peer-review groups to help others share their views.

Danny, understanding that change is just a part of the industry, decided his time was better spent dealing directly with clients. He would take the updates from many of the advisory committees and show his clients how his solutions and the work of his company would be better than what the regulations were asking for. Danny spent a lot of time and energy talking to his community of clients, discussing the future and how his company was positioning itself to be a leader in the industry. While his clients were surely grateful for the information, it didn't really generate awareness with other parts of the community.

If we look at the two companies right now, we can see how the picture of leadership is building. Ricky's company is starting to develop a sphere of influence that includes many different industries and a more national or even global focus. Danny's company is very focused on his accomplishments and is developing a strong relationship with his client base. Ricky is active in the process of developing the future of his industry, while Danny is in a reactive position. Let's continue:

Ricky was plugged in to some of the committees that were influencing policy decisions in his market. Understanding how some of the new regulations were going to be enacted, he started working with different software vendors to innovate new ways to deliver great service and products to the marketplace. He began partnering with some of the best technology companies and started creating deeper networks that would look to his operation for help when the regulations did change.

Danny, reacting to some of the changes coming up, tried to anticipate the needs of his clients. He created new solutions that benefited his customer base, but that were not widely accepted in the national market. Since he was creating very specific solutions, getting support and technical help was difficult. Instead he was forced to hire technical people because so many of the new processes he created required elaborate in-house development. When he looked for guidance from other professional sources, he found that he had strayed far enough out of the norm for his industry that there just wasn't as big of a network for him to rely on for advice and support.

At industry conferences there were several times when both Ricky and Danny were in attendance. Ricky was very open with his competitors about what his company was doing and how they were building success. Danny learned to be very closed off about his company. He used these opportunities as covert operations to try and discover what the competition was doing. While Ricky was building trust and a community of like-minded business owners, Danny was continuing to position himself on the outside fringes of the industry.

I could go on about the differences between the business owners and ultimately the success of their businesses, but I think you get the idea. In the three-year period of time that I was dealing with these two business owners, Ricky grew to become one of the most influential people and businesses in the industry and had a bottom line to prove it. Danny continued to struggle to develop a market for his services outside of his local community.

The lesson to be learned by these two businesses is that market leadership is about how well you are able to influence all parts of your industry. How involved are you in all aspects of the industry? Are you developing a company that is ready to be a market leader?

One of the main reasons that Ricky was so successful at positioning himself as a market leader is that he spent a great deal of time preparing his company to be able to handle the pressures of being a leader. By making sure his staff was certified, he told the market and all his potential customers that everyone, not just him, was qualified to help. He invested heavily in providing top-notch technology to his office to make sure his staff was able to provide the best in products and service. The leadership value was shared by everyone at the company.

Apply these lessons to your business. Consumers have more choices than ever when deciding how to spend their money. Your company, and by extension you, are going to be thoroughly researched before any of your prospects turn into customers. People are afraid of losing their money to someone that isn't credible. So your first lesson is to inspire trust.

Trust comes from sharing your authentic self. Jeffrey Gitomer (www. buygitomer.com) is a sales master, and he has this wonderful saying: "All things being equal, people would rather buy from their friends." It applies to leadership, too. People will follow you if they believe they know the real you. If you aren't being genuine with others, you will have a hard time leading them.

In the previous example, Ricky put a huge focus on training his staff and getting them certified. This is one of the best ways to build trust in your market. You don't have to know everything in your market, but you do have to show your market that you have a commitment to learning. To expand that trust, find ways to share the knowledge you gain with your clients.

Building trust means acting in a responsible way. Admitting you're wrong is a difficult thing for many businesses to do. When you make a mistake, you have two choices: admit it and move on, or make a complete mess of everything. Building trust and being a leader means that you admit your mistakes, make an effort to resolve them, and you move on. If you choose to do anything else, you will lose the respect and trust of your customers.

The second lesson is to inspire action. Ultimately, you are looking for your customers to take the action of buying from you. But the idea here is to inspire others. In order to do this, you need to give value to the market. The key word in that sentence is *give*.

I worked for a fairly successful business owner who would consistently talk about the value beyond the sale. He talked to his sales staff about it at every meeting. Anyone can sell a widget. What value are you giving to your customers beyond the product or service? Don't think for one minute that you can sell value. Think about the extended warranties that are offered at electronics stores. How often have you purchased a product and then been sold on the extended warranty? It's great for the store. Some of those warranties can double the profit margin on those products. But as a consumer, how do you feel after you have purchased a warranty? Are you grateful to the store, or do you walk out a little upset that you spent far more than you had planned?

Some stores offer to fix problems for free. If given the choice, most people would buy from the store offering free service—not because they got something for free, but because they felt like they were being treated more fairly at that store.

Think of ways you can give value to others in your market. Don't limit yourself to thinking only of your customers. Remember, there are so many other stakeholders in each market. How can you help your suppliers? How can you help trade associations or membership groups? One of the best ways to provide leadership to a market is to share your knowledge with these types of groups. Go to trade shows and look for ways that you can give value to others. Be remembered for what you gave to others, not for what you took from them.

The final lesson to think about in leading a market is to be visible and available. There is a big difference between leadership and celebrity. In our "reality TV" lives, we've blurred those lines a little. Be very careful that you don't cross that line. It is hard enough to find the time necessary to run a successful business. So what would happen to your time if you were being pulled in multiple directions—promoting your celebrity self and your business? Even if you were able to get the marketing benefit of constantly being in the public eye, you will need to maintain that authenticity that you are a hard worker and building a strong and successful business.

Being visible and recognizable can be a seductive feeling. It's easy to start to think about your personal brand instead of how to lead your market. As much as we elevate them in our society, celebrities are not leaders. Don't strive to be a celebrity or a famous business owner unless you are ready to turn over the management of your business to someone else. Don't dream about a celebrity lifestyle unless you are ready to give up the role of business owner. Instead, use your leadership to shape your market and build an amazing business. Put the focus where it belongs. Stay accessible to others in your market. Don't get bigger than your business, and you'll always have room to grow.

6

Why can't my employees get along with each other?

Because They Don't Trust You, Your Company, Management, Or Each Other.

I s there a constant stream of complaining employees walking into your office? Has your HR department installed the DMV "Take a Number" policy? Are you having more meetings about the proper way to handle conflict in the office than on business strategy? Does it feel like you are running a day care rather than a professional office?

It would be easy for me to write down (once again) that it's all your fault. You have failed as a leader, a business owner, and as a person. The employees are right: you are not worthy of their infinite talents. Well, maybe that's going a little too far. If you've got an unhappy team, you are going to have to accept that you played some part in that. But what I've found is that when employees start fighting with each other, it's more about their lack of faith and trust than it is about your leadership style.

Sometimes—and I know this is hard to believe, but it is true—some people just don't get along with each other.

Now, you can't control whether or not your employees are going to like each other on a personal level. There will always be petty jealousies, ambitious twits, and manipulative jerks in the workforce. Oh, and did I mention brownnosers? Yes, there will always be someone waiting to kiss your ass in the hopes of getting a raise, promotion, or better assignment.

But what you can control is how you, your management team, and your company treat your employees. Employees will put up with all the negativity spewed by other team members as long as they can trust the direction of the company. As long as they believe their voices will be heard, hard work will be rewarded, and good will defeat evil then they will put up with a mountain of bullshit from their coworkers. The minute they lose that trust in the company, all hell will break loose, and you are going to have a major employee problem on your hands.

Now comes the part where you tell me all about your employee-recognition program. How you recognize and reward an employee every month for meeting some objective. You will tell me about the different potlucks your employees do each month and how everyone is recognized on his or her birthday with a card and maybe even a small party. You might have even gone so far as to create special bonus programs, where an employee can "earn" rewards through good behavior.

But just like in relationships, the rewards and perks end up needing to be more elaborate and expensive in order to generate excitement. After a while, employees start rolling their eyes about all the "recognition." They complain that the wrong person won the award. The cake that was brought in for a birthday party had the wrong frosting. They complain that the company is trying too hard. A program that was supposed to inspire becomes an ironic joke. At some point, the costs start outweighing the benefits, and the program slows down or stops. Nothing will kill trust between you and your employees faster than giving them something and then taking it back. Even if it was something they didn't want to begin with.

Too often, companies will start a recognition program without doing much research. I really believe that most business owners go into the program with the best of intentions. You really are trying to give your employees a little extra recognition, because, hey, we all like to feel special, and you want to provide a little motivation to inspire others to work just a bit harder.

The only problem is that these types of programs only appeal to a small portion of the population. It's sad, because these are the people who work hard and are constantly working to improve themselves. Sad not because these are the only people who get rewarded, sad because this is becoming such a small part of our society. Too many people are expecting everything to be handed to them. They are expecting to win employee of the month simply because they showed up every day. And then these are the same people who complain the loudest when someone who works hard every day is rewarded. Sad.

So if you decide a rewards program is right for your company, here are a few guidelines to keep in mind. First, make sure it is sustainable. Whatever you decide to offer needs to be something you believe you can commit to for the entirety of your business's existence. As in forever. The only changes allowed would be to offer more, never less. Next, make sure the program is based solely on objective measurements—sales per month, clients served, calls taken, invoices collected, etc. Whenever you leave something open to a subjective opinion, you open your company up to favoritism complaints. Finally, don't limit it to a single recipient. Whoever meets their objective goal in a month can win it. In essence, you could be giving out the reward or recognition to every single employee every month. You won't, but if the program is designed right, it could be possible.

But it doesn't have to be that complicated. Most employees who are unhappy at work aren't upset about the recognition program. Employees who become disgruntled with management cite lack of communication as the number-one reason. The second complaint is a lack of leadership. In truth, they are one and the same. It is the role of the leader to make sure everyone in the organization understands the direction of the company. Communicating your vision is where you will start building momentum.

How do managers communicate? They like to talk in formal meetings. Most managers are ambitious enough to want to get a bigger job, fancier office, and more people reporting to them. There is a little arrogance and conceit that goes with that, so these people will spend every moment they can listening to themselves speak. It's funny to sit in a meeting and watch these people do everything they can to get the last word in. They don't care about the leadership; they care about the appearance of being important.

Entrepreneurs, leaders, communicate fast and furious. They don't have time for formal meetings; if they see a person in the hallway they have a discussion right then and there. Reports, predictability, and consistency are things other people are hired to worry about. As a leader, it's about the vision and the mission. But this "hurry up and go" mentality can be mistaken as you not caring about the thoughts and opinions of others.

So meetings happen, but nothing ever happens in a meeting.

Don't let decisions die in committee. Good ideas have a way of getting lost in meetings. Too many people find faults in the details, and in the end the decision always seems to be "do more research." That is another way of saying, "No one really wants to say no to the idea, but then again, no one really wants to do it either." All you want to do is reward action. If it was at all possible, you'd avoid the committee and get on with the work of building the business. But someone, somewhere, said leadership and good management require you to let everyone have a say and get "buy-in" before a decision is made.

Unless everyone is in agreement (and honestly, when has that ever happened?), you are going to have a fractured team where someone is going to believe his or her opinion doesn't matter. And that's when the backstabbing party begins. Meetings might be the biggest waste of time and effort in the business world. Want to test the effectiveness of your meetings? Remove all of the chairs from your meeting room. This isn't exactly a new idea, but it is very effective. When the comforts of the meeting room are gone, your people will get to the point quickly.

The next time you have a meeting, let someone else take the lead. Change your focus in the meeting. Rather than paying attention to the message, look at how everyone is communicating with each other. Are the employees asking questions and getting complete answers (notice I said complete, not approved or acceptable)? Is the content of the meeting meaningful to everyone in the room? Would you accept meetings like this as the only communication you got about your business? Chances are the answers are no to all of these questions, and you are going to have a new perspective on how to measure the quality of a meeting.

Communication needs to be about more than just a monthly "state of the business" meeting. In fact, one of the ways to improve communication is to reduce or even eliminate meetings. I know that sounds totally backward, but there are so many different ways to communicate with your team that meetings are becoming obsolete. One of the biggest wastes of time is sitting in a conference room listening to two people debate the good and bad points of ideas that have very little to do with the bottom line.

Utilize e-mail and Web-conferencing technology as much as you can to handle important details. Communicate as directly and openly as you can with all of your employees. If you make a decision, tell everyone not just the decision, but the reasons you chose to go in that direction. No one has to agree with you, but if people understand why you made a decision, they are more likely to support it. If they still think it's necessary, leave procedural meetings to your management team so they can figure out how they are going implement these new strategies. Your meetings should be reserved for closing deals and announcing major news to your employees.

Which follows to the next point: don't over schedule yourself. As a leader you need to be seen and heard often. It is too easy to get caught up in projects or sales calls or other events that keep you from being visible to your employees. Even though you know what your schedule looks like, the perception from your staff is that you are never around. In order to build trust, you must be there with your employees.

Keep your schedule open for at least five to ten hours each week. Use this time to walk around and talk to your staff. Make unannounced client calls to check in and get feedback. Jump on the front lines and work with your staff for an hour or two. While it may not seem like a productive use of your time, it makes you seem more approachable. Employees who feel comfortable talking to you are going to trust you and your motives more readily.

Changing the culture of an organization is not as simple as flipping a light switch. It is going to take a strong commitment at all levels in order to be successful. Take a look at the trust levels in your organization. Are your managers constantly micromanaging their employees? Are your company policies written for adults, or are they written as if you employ school-age kids? Your employees will be looking for the hidden message in everything that you and your management team do. Make sure you are acting from a position of trust when you are dealing with your employees.

At some point sooner or later, every company has to deal with unhappy customers. I have spent a lot of time in customer-service organizations. As far as I can tell, they have all hired adults. In fact, they have all hired adults who have purchased something in the past. Out of all these purchases, every single one of these employees has been unhappy with something and even tried to return it. In other words, we've all been on the customer side of the equation when a product needs to be returned. But even with all this real-world experience, I have not found very many companies that are willing to trust their employees to simply handle the return.

There are entire returns departments. If someone wants a refund, it almost always takes "management approval." As if the manager has more experience and knowledge about taking back a product and returning the customer's money. Sure, there's a business reason for it all. But what does it say to your front-line employee? "I don't trust you enough to make the right decision when an unhappy customer shows up." That's certainly one way to show how much you trust your employees.

I worked in customer service at one company that authorized us to give up to a 10 percent discount on the customer's next order without management approval. We were told that it was a way for us to try to handle issues immediately with our customers and that we should use our best judgment during those situations.

It wasn't a big discount, but it solved a couple of problems. Right away, as employees we felt empowered by the management team. We could act with some autonomy. The customers also were able to get some immediate satisfaction without the hassle of trying to get a manager. Trust was being built three ways—management to employee, employee to management, and company to customer. Even though we had the power to offer a discount, many times employees would get creative and find other alternatives to satisfy the customer. Without feeling that trust from the company, these customer-service people would have never felt comfortable making this type of effort.

How you treat your employees will gauge how likely they are to trust you. Employees get discouraged rather easily. I work with a lot of people who are trying very hard to get promotions and advance their careers. One of the biggest complaints they share is that promotions never go to the right person. It just goes to show most employees have a very narrow view of the organization. They see everything through their own personal lens. Whom you hire, fire, promote, and reprimand is your own business, and generally you don't need to explain yourself. But understand that how you act in these circumstances affects many more people in your organization than the person you are dealing with. Promoting someone to a new position is great for her, but it could cause hard feelings among everyone else if she isn't seen as qualified to hold the position. Firing someone who is well liked and productive can have an equally negative effect on your team.

You must remember that when dealing with employees, treating them fairly doesn't always mean treating them equally. Each employee is a unique person with specific skills and abilities. To think that each person will respond the same way to an action is foolish. Get to know your employees. Learn about their desires, their fears, what their goals are. Not everyone is motivated by the same things. While one person may be delighted about public praise, another person may get very embarrassed by it.

One word of caution, though. When it comes to the rules of the office, whether it is the dress code or showing up on time, you need to provide a consistent response. Letting certain people bend or even break the rules will create morale difficulties down the road. Even if you think it is justified based on an employee's position or contribution to the company, you must apply these standards equally across all employees.

If you didn't already know this, you will find the biggest distractions to employees is the potential for layoffs or rumors of a person being fired. Many times these things simply can't be avoided. If the time should ever come when you have to make the decision to lay off staff, do it quickly and decisively. Don't let this drag out over months or even weeks. If you can, make your evaluations in private, and then make your changes. The longer you drag it out, the more damage you inflict on the morale of your remaining employees. You will also create a cutthroat, every-man-for-himself atmosphere in the office if everyone believes he or she could be the next to go.

If you need to fire someone, do it quickly and base it on a specific action. Send the message to your team that certain behaviors simply won't be tolerated. Yes, it is difficult, and yes, it affects morale. But don't get trapped into thinking you have to hold on to someone who is a bad fit simply because he is a good person or has a difficult personal life. You can't let anything but the job at hand affect your decision making. It's hard, it's cold, but unfortunately, it's also your business.

In general, layoffs are more destructive to employee morale than firings. When someone is fired, the majority of the team knew it was coming. Heck, even the person getting fired usually knew it was coming. But layoffs are different. Layoffs are unpredictable, and they are a reflection of the overall performance of the business. In fact, it's a report card on how well you are leading your business. If you have to announce layoffs, your employees will question whether or not the business will survive, if they will have a job, and who will still be here when it's all done. Employees may complain about communication the most, but layoffs are certainly the most destructive thing you can do.

I've heard a lot of theories about employee turnover. Some people talk about the overall costs of training a new person as a reason to avoid layoffs. Others talk about needing to purge the bottom 10 percent of your staff each year in order to keep the staff motivated.

I'm not sure what the right answer is. What I do know is that bad employees are a disease and need to be removed. Good employees are the strength of the company and need to be nurtured. I also know that negativity spreads faster than positivity, so be sure you are keeping an eye out for those employees who are going to cause a problem. Do not hesitate to remove them. Don't wait for the end of the year, and don't worry about the costs of hiring someone new. The damage of an unhappy worker outweighs all of that.

It's easy to get caught up treating your employees like children when they spend so much time every day acting like children. But remember, they are acting like children because they don't feel like you respect them as adults, and maybe you don't. In order to build a better working environment, at some point one of you is going to have to reach out and show that kind of respect and trust to the other. Would you recognize it if it was offered to you? Probably not, because if you are like most business owners I know, it's not that big of a priority compared to all of the other issues you are dealing with. But when things start falling apart in the workplace, it will consume all of your time. Instead of allowing things to boil over later, why not take the time to step back and realize you have a very capable workforce filled with responsible adults, and start treating them like it? Maybe, just maybe, they'll start acting like it, and you will have a workforce that not only trusts you but might show you a little loyalty on the side.

7

Why Do We Spend So Much On Advertising And Get So Little In Return?

Because Your Advertising Sucks.

When advertising is done right, it always generates more revenue than it cost to produce. Always. That's the sign of a good advertisement. I know your ads suck because if they worked, you would run them everywhere and have more business than you could deal with. The biggest misconception out there about advertising is that the advertisement needs to be constantly changing to keep it fresh. Trust me, some of the most profitable ads have run for years without a single change to them.

So if you are asking why you are spending so much on advertising, then you obviously have not found an ad that works. And if you are pinching pennies on your ad budget, then you are not going to ever find an ad that works. Don't focus on the cost. Focus on the effectiveness of the advertisements. When you create your ads based on how much they cost you, then you are guaranteed to continue creating ads that suck.

Marketing is a very unique business skill and is often overlooked by business owners. And please do not confuse marketing and advertising. They are not the same thing! You need to educate yourself as much as possible in marketing. Marketing is the process of identifying prospective customers and drawing their interest to your business. Advertising is a tool in the marketing process—and it is typically the most costly tool you can use.

When you develop your marketing plan, advertising is going to have a prominent place at the top of the plan. Advertising is the most recognized way to get your message out to the market and to let prospective buyers know where to find you. But the world of advertising is rapidly changing, and it is getting harder and harder to create effective ads.

While the massive growth of technology over the past twenty years has completely reshaped most marketing strategies, it has been the increase in availability of that technology that has transformed advertising. As more people are able to use computers, phones, and tablets to access stories on the Internet, there is less need for printed words. With news aggregators on the Web, people can now consume the information they want without sorting through any of the filler they don't care about. Talk about a game changer for the newspaper industry.

We've already seen the decline of several major papers in the United States. Many others are moving to an online-only model. Subscriptions are falling every year, which means the papers are even more dependent on ad revenue to stay open. As ads fill up the pages, there is less room on the paper for real content. As readers get tired of buying a newspaper that is more advertisement and less news, they drop their subscriptions. And a horrible cycle emerges.

With less subscribers, the newspapers need to get even more advertisers into the paper. But that same drop in the subscriber base will make the advertising less effective, meaning businesses that normally advertised may start to drop off. It's an unfortunate truth, but the traditional newspaper industry is already dead. It just hasn't pulled the plug yet.

At its best, the Internet provides real-time information about stories worldwide. It gives everyone fair access to the same information, retailers, products, services, and opinions. At its worst, it is a melting pot of half truths, uninformed opinions, and biased stories. But in an era where newspapers are dying or dead, it is the obvious replacement for people to get their news.

But quality advertising on the Web still has a way to go. Even the best constructed advertisements are too easy to ignore on a given Web site. Those you can't ignore are typically so distracting that they work against the company producing them and the Web site that decided to host them. Not exactly the best use of your marketing dollars.

Radio and television have been stalwarts of advertising for decades. Where a print ad has to appeal to the eyes, radio and TV can provide the additional staying power of sound. But radio has always suffered from the drive-time dilemma. Most people listen to the radio in the car, not at home or in the office. So any ad they hear in the car has to have enough staying power to survive until your audience reaches their destination. On TV, technology and choice are reducing the effectiveness of ads for small businesses. Streaming and recording services allow viewers to skip ads all together. Those viewers who can't skip the commercials tend to flip channels looking for alternate programming.

So what does it all mean? Should you give up on advertising? Is it hopeless to ever get an ad that works? Absolutely not! But if you are going to get your advertising up to par, you need to get some high-quality help with it. Strong, tested ads can pull in new customers and new revenue. Just don't turn the process over to the creative person in the office and hope it will be good enough.

Before you create your ads, make sure you have a good idea who your ideal customer is. Being able to target your audience is an absolute must for effective advertising. Don't get lazy and comfortable on this part. You need to know more than just the demographics of your ideal customers. What types of magazines do they like to read? What are their hobbies? Do they have common interests?

With in-depth knowledge about your customers, you will have a better chance of getting your message to them in ways they are ready to accept it. Show them that you understand the problems they are facing and that you have a solution, and you'll be able to get twice the response as any ad you've placed, ever.

Make sure your ads are set up so that you can test and track their performance. Testing isn't just about whether an ad works or not. You need to know if a certain type of publication works better than another. Are there key words that are more effective? Are people more likely to e-mail or call from an ad you place? Is blue or green a better color to get a response? You need to become an expert in your ads and why they work or don't work. You can only do that by testing the response to your ads.

When you are creating your ad, there are five essential components that must be addressed. First is the headline. It has to jump off the page at the reader. But here's the catch with a headline: a mediocre or bad headline means no one will read the ad, and a great one means someone will read your ad. Notice I didn't say a great one will generate a sale—its purpose is to get your audience to read your copy.

The copy in your ad can either be long and informative or short and clever. Either way it has to deliver a punch to the reader. Your copy is your only opportunity to provide your proof to a prospective customer. Can you really do what you say you can do? Why should I use you instead of your competitor? You can talk all you want about how great your product is, but if you can't prove it by overcoming my objections with your copy, you will lose me. This is the biggest reason you are going to want to bring in professional help. Anyone can think of a clever headline, but writing great copy is best left to the experts.

The third thing every ad must have is a strong call to action. An ad that says "Hi there, how are you, I'm awesome" is not going to do any good. You need an ad that says "Hey there, I'm awesome, call me and I'll prove it." A call to action can be as simple as setting a deadline for a phone call or an e-mail. Or it could be creative like having prospects go to your Web site and download a free whitepaper or eBook in exchange for their e-mail address. The important thing is to get your prospects to act on the information they see in your ad.

Whether you want to believe it or not, imagery and color have a huge impact on the success of an advertisement. I spent a lot of years fighting this point with several marketing people. It just didn't make sense to me that colors created emotional responses in readers. That blue portrayed a business as dependable while orange made the business seem whimsical and fun. To me the ad was all about the content. But I've been converted. A good friend of mine showed me the data from his own advertising tests. Color and imaging can have a huge effect on your potential buyers.

If you insist on choosing your own colors and images, be smart about it. Stick with muted colors that will look good printed on plain paper. Don't count on your ads getting the glossy treatment. A good rule of thumb is if a color was popular in the eighties, it probably doesn't belong in your advertisements. Also, when you are picking images, don't try to go artsy or cute. Pick images that represent what your company does. This, of course, is the safe route for do-it-yourselfers. If you want neon-green colors and a snowflake to represent your commitment to the environment, you'll probably want to let a pro design that one (and maybe listen to a few of their suggestions).

Finally the most important thing your ads must have is the word FREE. There is no other word like it in the advertising dictionary. It is the power word that does more for your success rate than anything else. This is not anything groundbreaking for sure. We all know that *free* is advertising gold. What you may not know is that *free* comes with a down side—it creates skepticism. Since everyone knows *free* is essential in advertisements, your customers will look at your *free* offer and try to figure out the catch.

So *free* is not going to be enough. You are going to need to add two more words to your ad—*no obligation*. Help your potential customers break free of their skepticism by letting them know they are under no obligation to buy or do anything after the *free* offer. And then, most importantly, you have to mean it!

Your advertising is a means to get people to come to you, instead of you chasing them down. Building a successful ad is pretty straightforward, but it has to mean something to your market. When you offer something for free, you are going to get them to come to you. That is your chance to prove your skill and your character. Don't miss out on it.

Don't forget, advertising is only a part of your marketing plan. If you are trying to make advertising your entire marketing process, consider what you are asking your ads to do. Whether they are in print or online, you are expecting a handful of words and a picture to be your entire sales team. You're expecting these ads to find your prospects, convince them to buy from you, and then lead them to your business to complete the transaction. It won't happen, and you'll be back here again asking why you are wasting so much money on ads that don't work. Advertising is an important part of growing your business, but it can't be the all-encompassing focus of your marketing efforts.

8

Why Is Our Entire Marketing Budget Focused On Something Called Brand Awareness?

Because You Have A Lazy Idiot In Charge Of Your Marketing.

Maybe I'm just bitter because I didn't think of this first. As a consultant, I spend an enormous amount of time focused on results. And not just my own results, but those of the company that hired me. It's measurable: how much additional revenue was generated, how well costs were contained, what the profit margin increase was, how much we improved productivity. This is how my success is measured.

But these "brand-awareness" guys are flat-out amazing. They readily admit you can't measure the effectiveness of their work. They spend money on advertising that is intentionally designed without a call to action. These promos are guaranteed to not bring in any money, and yet these marketing geniuses not only keep their jobs but get raises and bigger budgets.

Let that sink in. Your brand-awareness guy is spending your money so that people remember the name of your business. The goal of the strategy is to make sure potential customers think about your company first when (if) they ever decide to buy your products. "It's an investment in future sales," you will hear them tell you. In the meantime, you are paying a salary to someone in marketing and sales that is producing no income, spending dollars on advertising that doesn't create revenue, and managing a budget for a strategy that is intentionally putting off results until "sometime" in the future.

Don't believe me? Ask your brand-awareness guy to prove his results. How many words does it take for him to get out an answer? How many "ifs" and "buts" do you get? How many times does he say you don't understand what he is doing and that this is a long-term strategy that can't be measured in the short term? How nervous does he get when you put deadlines or sales quotas on him? If you have a brand-awareness guy (or girl) in charge of your marketing, you have been wasting money and will continue to do so until you replace him or her.

Marketing is the single most important and misunderstood part of your business. I went to Amazon and searched for "marketing" in the book section. There were 555,039 results! There cannot possibly be half a million theories on marketing, but I guess if you had enough time you could read all those books and find out. What it really says is that marketing is necessary and no one is doing it right.

When we talk about the momentum of a company, marketing is the catalyst. It is the engine that drives your business to success or failure. Marketing is a simple concept: get the right message to the right people when they are ready to buy. Easy, right?

This is not a marketing book, and I am not going to cover marketing basics in this chapter. If you need help with the basics or you just don't understand marketing, study up on it. Or better yet, hire someone who understands it and let him or her do the work (just make sure this person isn't a marketing "guru" promising magic through brand awareness).

The most dangerous idea that a business owner can hold on to is that marketing and sales are the same thing. Marketing and sales work hand in hand, and it is because they are so tied together that many people talk about them as if they are the same thing. This is why so much money is wasted every year in the name of marketing. When your marketing is working at peak performance, it is generating a steady stream of leads. Your sales team, when it is working at peak performance, is converting those leads into paying customers. They work together, but they aren't a substitute for each other.

While they are two different functions, they do have the same goal: create revenue. Think about your latest marketing campaign and the last set of advertisements you created. How much revenue was generated from your marketing? Take a minute and write down the numbers. If you aren't going to take five minutes to write it down because the numbers are embarrassing, that should tell you something about your marketing. If you won't do it because you think it's a waste of time, that should tell you something about your opinion of marketing research. Write it down; I guarantee you the rest of the book will still be here when you're done. Make two columns on a piece of paper, and total up the amount of money you spent on marketing; then use the other column to write down the revenue you generated from each marketing piece. (You are tracking the leads you get from each marketing source, right?)

If you are like most businesses, you are wasting money every month on marketing activities that do nothing to bring in revenue. How are you supposed to build any kind of consistent revenue if you are wasting money on activities that do nothing to create new sales? We will talk about how to maximize your sales soon; right now we are going to fix your most glaring marketing problems.

Your marketing is not a replacement for your sales team. Don't ever mistake a flyer, a Web site, a logo, or a business card for a salesperson. To build revenue, you need to understand what marketing can and cannot do for you. The whole purpose of marketing is to drive traffic to your business. You want a flood of potential customers coming to you and asking questions. That is marketing at its finest. Marketing cannot be your entire sales force. A flyer cannot make calls to prospects. A business card cannot close a deal or sign a contract.

This is one of the biggest traps business owners fall into. You can hold on to the tangible marketing product. You can see it, and you can hand it out. You can mail it, and it has all of those properties that make you feel like each piece is going to generate a bunch of new sales. So you spend a little more money on the product to make it really stand out. You put all kinds of contact information on it, and maybe you even include an order form. But are you really ever getting your investment back? Marketing doesn't make the sale; it drives traffic to your sales team.

There are very few people in this world who truly understand how to market products and services. But there are hundreds of thousands of people selling themselves as marketing experts, and their only credentials are taking a marketing class, reading a marketing article, or spending a year or two working in a marketing role. These people may know the right buzzwords and may have some artistic or creative talent, but they are not marketers.

True marketers are focused on one thing only—generating revenue. Everything they do is based around your products and your message and creating urgency for your prospective customers to act now. These professionals know how to identify and capture the attention of your audience. If you find one of these special people, hold on to him or her.

But how do you identify the good from the rest? I use what I call the brand-recognition test. If you are interviewing a marketing person and she starts talking about the importance of generating brand recognition, you can be sure she doesn't have your revenue on her mind. Brand recognition is one of the buzz words that has gained a lot of traction lately. It is to the point now that people have just accepted it as a necessary part of the marketing experience.

What is brand recognition besides a big waste of your money? It is the use of ads, marketing pieces, radio spots, sponsorships, etc., to generate awareness of your company. You are spending money so that people in your community feel comfortable that you are a trustworthy brand. While it is a noble thought and certainly has its place, it doesn't generate momentum for your business.

There was a movie in 1993 called *Dave* in which a normal guy who looks like the president of the United States ends up standing in for him after the real president suffers a stroke. As the movie unfolds, Dave starts looking at the budget and runs across a line item for an advertising campaign. This campaign is designed to make the American people feel better about their purchase of an American-built car.

In one of the classic lines of the movie, Dave says, "I don't want to tell some eight-year-old kid he's gotta sleep in the street because we want people to feel better about their car. Do you want to tell them that?" Whenever I hear people talk about brand recognition, this is the image that comes to my mind.

If you are currently spending money on this type of marketing, stop. Let's boil this down into really simple terms. Since brand recognition is the process of getting a community of people to know that you exist, many times the money that is being spent is on products that have no sales message or call to action. In other words, your money is being spent on marketing messages that have no chance of inspiring your customers to buy from you right now. This is easily justified by the marketing team with another buzz-worthy phrase: top of mind.

Top of mind refers to potential buyers thinking of your company and your products first when they are ready to buy. So, in essence, your marketing dollars are being spent to make people who don't want your product and aren't ready to buy your product think about you first if they ever decide they want to buy your product. And these are the marketing geniuses who get paid the big bucks. Now is the time to take a step back and ask yourself: What is my marketing budget really paying for?

If you have allowed your marketing to focus on "brand recognition" or "top of mind," then you need to accept the fact that you have adopted a very passive strategy that has no real hopes of creating immediate revenue. The only business this works for is the marketing company (or person) you hired. They are getting paid every time they create one of these new ads for you. Soon, you'll hear from your marketing team that you need to keep your marketing fresh, and you'll have to pay for a whole new message to be created, once again, to maintain brand awareness and develop top-of-mind recognition.

It's like throwing money out the window. When you are ready to start a true marketing campaign, you need to have a very focused idea of what you are trying to accomplish. Programs like the one I just described are easy to get involved in. To be honest, they make sense on the surface. When you are talking to a marketing company, it is very easy to get impressed by the sample ads they have. You look at the quality of the graphics and the clever words they use, and you can see how much better it is than anything you've come up with in the past.

But be careful. Graphics and quirky headlines don't always result in revenue. If you want to be impressed by a marketing company, talk to them about the final results of the campaign. Ask questions like how many new clients did this campaign generate? How quickly did the campaign pay off in terms of new sales? How many times did the client reorder the same advertising campaign to be run in different markets? Always focus your marketing efforts on revenue, not creativity.

I can remember when one of the companies I worked for early in my career tried to put together a marketing campaign. They called in several of the local marketing agencies to get their pitch. Each of the agencies came in with amazing portfolios. The ads were beautiful. Some of them were smart, others witty; you could close your eyes and imagine how well each of these agencies would deliver new sales.

Each of the presentations talked about creating a unique identity for the company. It included a new logo, new Web site, new colors, new letterhead, new envelopes, etc. Out of ten companies, two really stood out from the rest.

The first company talked about all of the identity things that everyone else brought up, but they had another section for a long-term advertising program. This program would be a monthly recurring fee, and it would generate new ads to be used in multiple outlets. It was designed to develop brand recognition!

The second company that stood out to me didn't come prepared with anything. The two representatives walked in with a pad of paper and a small folder of some examples. Instead of wowing us with their creativity, they peppered us with questions. What were our expectations? What made us special? Who were our customers? When they left, both sides knew they would not be working together.

The company I worked for instantly dismissed the second company. In our meeting room, they were derided for being unprepared and not understanding the industry. They were looked at as novices who were still learning about marketing. Later I found out that the marketing agency felt the same way about the company I worked for. We couldn't answer any of their questions. We had no idea about our market. And it was evident when the first company started taking our money.

Brand recognition is the worst form of lazy marketing. Because all the focus is on just getting your name out to the public, you stop thinking about the identity of your actual customer. Then it becomes a vicious cycle of waste. You don't get the results you need, so you spend more money to widen your advertising to new markets. Instead of focusing on the customer base you can help, you continue to water down your message so that it has broad appeal to everyone. Instead of standing out from the crowd, you become part of the nameless, faceless mob of companies competing for the same dollar. And the process begins again until you finally wake up, or you run out of money.

There is a better way, but you have to be willing to let go of these destructive marketing choices. Marketing is hard enough without creating the negative momentum that you find with these passive strategies. Shift your focus. Remember, every dollar you spend on marketing needs to return more than a dollar in sales. If your marketing gurus can't make that happen, replace them with someone who can.

I know it is never that simple. The focus of marketing has really shifted to the "brand." It's a shame that we've allowed this happen in business. In every other function of a company, the focus is on the customer. But in marketing, in the one department that should focus on satisfying customers' wants and needs, the focus is on the image of the company. It's no wonder revenue is down and the most common open position in the want ads is for commission sales. No one is selling anything!

If you want to sell something, get your marketing people focused on the customer. They should know everything about your ideal customer. This is the real work of marketing. In order to drive more traffic to your business, you need to understand who is buying from you, why they buy, when they need your products, and how they will use your products and services. The creative stuff may be more fun, and it may be more tangible, but it is the intimate knowledge of your customer that makes the sale.

Brand recognition is an effect of your marketing just like revenue. Most marketing gurus like to think of brand recognition as a cause rather than the effect. They try to use it as a way to generate sales, and it will never work like that. They aren't thinking about the true cause-and-effect relationship at work.

In fact, if you do your marketing the right way, you'll get brand recognition without ever having to buy it. You see, a funny thing happens when you get the right message to the right people. Your business delivers a great product, and you have happy customers. Do it for a little while, and you'll make a bunch of money and get the brand recognition your marketing guru was working so hard to get before.

9

What is the most important asset my company owns?

Your Customer Database.

I didn't always believe that to be true. It took a round-table discussion with several other business owners before I was able to see the light on this point. I was sitting in a small conference room with four other people. All five of us were business owners, and while we had all known each other and talked in the past, this was the first time we had all sat in the same room together.

This meeting of the minds was a way for all of us to get and give support and help each other stay focused on our businesses. During the course of the discussion, someone raised this question: "If you knew you were going to lose everything in your business except for one thing, what would be the one thing you would save?" It was a great question, and I wish it were something I had come up with.

Four different answers were offered: my employees, my customers, my product/intellectual property, and my insurance policy. We all had a good laugh about the insurance policy. Then the debate came down between product, employee, and customer.

The argument for product was based on a patented idea that hadn't quite been released. If it worked, it was a million-dollar idea, and it was the result of years of work for that business owner. But we had to relate it to all businesses, and would saving the products off a retail shelf be the most important thing in the business? All around the table we agreed products could be replaced.

"I have the absolute best team out there. Nothing gets done without my employees." This was the central argument in favor of saving the team. Whether you have good or mediocre employees (I mean, come on, you aren't really holding on to your bad employees, are you?), it is hard to get much done without a team behind you. And with the right team, you could build back your business fairly quickly. So there was promise with this argument.

When customers came up for debate, it started to get really heated. On one side there were those arguing that getting customers was part of business. As long as you had a product and a team, you could get new customers. On the other side were those arguing that a strong customer base was essential for business success. Without customers, nothing else mattered. The debate ran longer than we thought it would.

Eventually, one person at the table decided to end the debate. "If I were going to start over, the most important thing to me would be the names, addresses, phone numbers, and e-mail addresses of all my customers. No matter what I did next, I would want to be able to get in touch with all of them and let them know about it. There is nothing better than contacting a customer and letting him or her know what you are doing. There is nothing easier than selling to someone who is already comfortable buying from you. I could lose everything else, but if I had my customer database, I'd have a multimillion-dollar business again in no time." And that was how I learned that the most valuable asset you have is your customer database.

You may have a multimillion-dollar building or factory. You may have the patent on the most revolutionary gadget ever. You may have a unique service or recipe that makes you ten times better than your competition. But the long-term viability of your company is tied up in your customer database.

The first five years of a small business are the most critical. Most new businesses don't survive. There are many reasons why they don't make it, but once thing is clear. Businesses that survive have grown their customer base substantially over those five years. Is it the reason they were successful? In a roundabout way, yes.

If you aren't growing your customer base, your business simply won't survive long. And really, just about every action you take as a business owner and every action you expect your employees to take on behalf of your business is designed to grow the number of customers you have. You might not have thought about it like that, but it is true.

So why is it that so few businesses realize the value and importance of their customer database? Industries that rely heavily on direct, one-to-one sales typically place more importance on their customer data, if only to get more referrals and repeat sales. But what about other industries? How are you collecting customer information? How are you storing it? What are you doing with it?

More often than not, small businesses that are struggling have not put much time or thought into maintaining their customer database. Oh, they tend to have a name, maybe a phone number, sometimes an address on file. But unless there is a point-of-sale system in place that requires any more information, that'll be just about it.

Depending on the type of business, there may not even be any order history associated with each customer. How can you run your business not knowing what your customers like to order? How do you get repeat business if you don't know how to get in touch with your existing customers? But the fact remains: the majority of small-business owners do not pay as much attention to the quality of their customer database as they should.

Here is a test for your customer database. Try to run these reports: client list showing active and inactive, order history by week/month/year, customer mailing list, top 10 percent of customers based on retail volume. If you can do this, great. If you can't, fix it. But whether or not you can, the question now becomes is this even something you will continue to look at? I guess it depends on how much you want to grow your business.

All of your future revenue is based on your ability to get new customers or to convince your existing customers to buy something from you. Think about it—ALL OF YOUR FUTURE REVENUE. If you can point to anything else you have in your warehouse, showroom, Web store, or display case that will account for all of your future revenue, I will be shocked. Your customer database needs to be treated with much more respect than you have shown it.

What is the value of one of your customers? If you grab a sales report and point to the average sale per transaction, then you have no idea how important your customer database is. I know that someone who has purchased my books is much more likely to buy other training from me. Customers who have gone through my training are even more likely to hire me as a consultant or as a speaker for an event. All of these future sales are part of the value of a single customer. These are my future sales, my future revenue, and they all come from existing customers.

In order to build a strong customer database and therefore strong future sales, you need loyal customers. There are four markers you can use to gauge the loyalty of your customers: Are they buying regularly? Are they immune to the offers of competitors? Do they recommend you and your products? Are they buying across all of your product or service lines? At first glance, most business owners nod in agreement when they see this list. "Of course our customers like us. We have a great group of core customers who buy regularly." But do you really?

This is where CEOs, managers, and business owners really do the company a disservice. Too often, this group of decision makers is too far away from the sales process to really understand what is going on. They get so used to the accepted business axioms that they can sometimes forget to actually do the measurements. Think about this. A commonly accepted axiom says 80 percent of your revenue will come from 20 percent of your customer base. But generalizations like that just don't cut it. Don't guess at it. You need to have a system in place that ranks your customers based on their purchase history. How integrated are your customers in your product mix? Are they repeat buyers? You may find out that you are getting 75 percent of your revenue from only 5 percent of your customer base.

Imagine the strength your marketing and sales teams would have if they knew exactly who your top 5 percent were. You can cater the customer experience to these highly valuable consumers. Customer loyalty is about purchase behavior, and if you aren't measuring what your customers are buying, then you are way behind in this game. Too many business owners and managers talk about the entire company being responsible for customer service. They are missing the point entirely. The real truth and the real path to long-term growth belong to the company that understands everyone needs to be responsible for customer loyalty.

So again, what is the value of your customers? If you want to raise revenue quickly, figure out how to get more products in front of your existing customers, and encourage them to buy. It's very well-known that it is much easier to hold on to a customer than to go out and find a new one. So take the time to create a system that rewards your existing customers.

Make sure you find ways to provide exclusive content and offers to your customer base. Whether you create a newsletter or a private Web site, provide a way for your customers to find out what's going on at your business. If you have new products coming out, make sure your existing client base knows about it first. If you are going to offer a sale, offer it to your existing customers first. Treat them with care and respect, and watch your revenues grow.

If you have a great relationship with your customers, it is even easier to get testimonials and positive product reviews. Use this to your advantage. Nothing sells product faster than a great testimonial. Take care of your customers, and they will take care of you.

One final note, as you build up a high-quality database of your customers, remember the trust they have placed in you. Never, ever sell your list to anyone. If you find a product or service that you absolutely love and you think your customers could benefit, tell them about it. But don't sell your list to that company. Once you break that trust, you will never get it back again.

10

Why can't my sales team sell anything?

Because Your Sales Team Isn't Filled With Salespeople.

here are people who work in sales, and then there are salespeople. People who work in sales need a system. They need a list of leads. They scour every resource they can find in order to get a list of names and phone numbers. If you don't provide them the list, they complain that they aren't getting the tools to do their job. They spend their time making phone calls hoping to get a meeting. No one likes cold calling, but they are in sales and they know they have to do it. It's part of the work of sales—the spirit-breaking, mind-numbing, hateful work of building a sales pipeline. They play the numbers game. Eventually if they make enough calls, they know they will get at least one yes.

When the calls dry up and the pressure is on, they will beg for referrals from friends and family. Then they move on to your existing customers to see if they can get a reorder to help boost their volume. They do presentations and show up at networking events. They schmooze and they hustle, and at the end of the month they squeeze out their quota—barely. And everyone celebrates the strong performance of the sales team, as they met their quota again for however many months in a row. To me, this is a sad joke! But over and over, I get told this is what sales looks like.

Don't get me wrong, these people can be successful, but it's based on hard work and a little bit of luck. But watch out when they get tired of the work or decide they don't need to do it; their sales will fall, and so will the revenue for your business. Instead of an active sales force, you end up with a team full of order takers. A significant majority of people who work in sales fit this description, and it is one of the major roadblocks keeping your business from growing. It's not their fault; they are trying to carve out a living, and for the most part these people put a lot of effort into trying to make it work. It's just not something that comes easy to everybody. You have to decide if you are OK with that level of production or if you are ready for something better.

A salesperson, a real salesperson, just goes out and sells product. He can't help but sell. It's in his blood. Give him a sample of your product and an order form and watch him bring back an armful of leads and prospects that are ready to become customers.

Watching a real salesperson work is a magical thing to see. She has an aura around her that just attracts others. Where a person in sales works hard to build up a connection with a prospect, a salesperson makes a connection with an entire room almost instantly without much effort. Then she gives her prospects the opportunity to buy from her. The right salesperson can be the difference between the long-term success and the short-term struggles of your business.

So how do you get salespeople? You steal them.

I laugh when I hear someone in an administration job talk about job security when he or she is given more responsibility. There are only two positions in any company that have job security: the owner and the salesperson. A true salesperson, one who naturally brings in new business consistently, is never fired. So don't ever think you are going to hang out by the unemployment office and find your next sales superstar. That is living in a dreamland.

If you want a sales star, you are going to have to convince one to work for you and leave the company, products, and customers he or she currently has. Start making a list of the best salespeople you've met. The best place to look is through your vendor list. Obviously someone there was good enough to convince you to buy.

If you don't have any luck there, then get a little creative. Start making phone calls to different service providers. Find companies that have independent salespeople, and invite them in to hear their sales pitch. Don't worry about what industry they are in. You only care about whether or not they can sell. Do they have the ambition? The passion? Are they personable but still able to control the sales meeting? Face it, you are conducting the most effective interview of a salesperson out there. When you find someone who is great, then it's time to make your move. Get him or her hired and on your team, no matter what it takes.

If you have a sales staff, now is the perfect time to evaluate how effective they are. Salespeople sell. That is what they thrive on. You have to work hard to keep a good salesperson from selling. Look at your current sales force. What are they doing each day?

Think about how active each person in your sales department is on a daily or even hourly basis. How many of them are waiting for the phone to ring? How many of them come back from sales meetings empty-handed? Again, your sales and marketing dollars need to return more revenue to your business. If you are paying a salesperson who isn't selling, it's like throwing away marketing dollars on brand awareness. What are you really getting from that person?

Remember, the only measurement that counts in sales is increased long-term revenue. I put the "long-term" in there for a reason. If you only focus on sales today, you can get some pretty shady characters selling promises your company can't keep. You don't need that. A focus on increasing long-term revenue means your sales team will continually bring on new customers and treat them with respect. They will act honorably and in the best interests of your company. So measure the success of your team by increased revenue over the long term. Don't look at phone calls or meetings or prospects or mailers as some form of success for your sales team. It's about money in the door. Make sure they know that, too.

Your sales team is highly affected by momentum. When sales start building, they come in bunches. When things start to get lean, it can feel like no one can make a sale. You need to keep a tight watch on your sales staff and make sure the momentum is always moving in the right direction. When you have salespeople who just aren't making sales, you need to replace them.

I've heard lots of excuses for keeping bad salespeople on board. "They just need a little time to get used to the market." "This is a bad time of year for everybody." "With a little training, he can be a good sales person for us." "She's on commission; this will work itself out on its own." The problem is that a bad salesperson will never become a great salesperson. And waiting for someone to quit because he or she failed to make a sale is a bad example to set. Don't let your sales staff take a step backwards. Get rid of the ones who don't sell and reward the ones that bring in revenue.

I worked with a small-business owner who was struggling to generate enough sales to support her business. She was placing local ads each month in the newspaper and attending several networking events. Her staff included six salespeople, half of whom were making regular but not spectacular sales.

What she couldn't understand was why her sales never grew. The company provided a very effective weight-loss system, which was a very in-demand product. After a few days of talking to her sales team and reviewing her marketing materials, I noticed several issues.

The first problem was that none of the sales team was actively prospecting. These were the typical order takers. They waited for the phone to ring or for someone to walk in the door before they sold anything. They knew their product and had a strong belief in it but just didn't know how to consistently get customers to spend their money on it. They also didn't do a single thing to find new customers.

This strategy isn't always effective, but it can work if the marketing strategy is sound and you have a team of closers. But when I reviewed the advertisements from the past few months, I could see there was a big problem. Each ad had different graphics and used different language, but they all told the same story. The ads talked about the history of the business, the quality of the product, and where to go to buy it. These were large, full-color, very expensive ads, and there was no offer or call to action and certainly no urgency. There also wasn't any type of emotional appeal. It was all rooted in the science behind why the product worked.

I tagged along to a networking event, and it was more of the same. Every conversation was about the logical benefits of the product. There were no personal stories, no emotional pulls, just a list of the technical research proving the product worked.

When the sales team came in the next day, I asked them to provide me with a personal success story they'd had with the product. Not surprisingly the three successful salespeople each had a great story. The other three couldn't come up with one between them.

I suggested a few fixes. Number one, I suggested a new team of salespeople. The owner needed an active sales staff that was motivated to generate new revenue. I also talked about changing the ads she was currently doing and adding more channels like radio and possibly doing tradeshows and workshops. I was met with a lot of resistance. The bottom line was that the business was surviving on what it was currently doing. She was not going to change everything just to get a few more sales each month.

Maybe you as a small business owner can relate. It's easy to believe your marketing is high quality and doing the job for you. But look at it with a careful eye. When you run your ads, do you see an immediate increase in traffic? Are you selling your products and services at full price or only when you discount them? Are you struggling month to month, or is your business enjoying an abundance of revenue? Your marketing and sales strategy either works or it doesn't. There is no room for a third option.

For my weight-loss friend, we made some minor changes. We used the same advertising dollars to create smaller ads and ran them more frequently. Every ad called on customers to come to the store for a free sample. The sales process was changed to focus on the transformation the product created. Before and after pictures along with their success stories were strategically placed in the store.

With a few other tweaks and some coaching with the sales staff, we were able to create an amazing campaign that jumped revenue by 10 percent in the first month. The moral of the story is to get active with your marketing if you want to get better results. Change up what you are doing, and make your message work for you. The momentum you build will carry you to higher revenues and ultimately greater profits.

Remember, your marketing is about generating traffic and leads to your sales team. A lazy sales team will wait until the marketing does all the work for them. If they don't get a sale, they are going to blame you for not giving them the support they needed to be successful. Accountability is a lost art anymore. Get rid of a lazy sales team.

Real salespeople understand they have a role to play in the marketing of your business. They are out in the community getting your message to everyone within earshot. Your marketing flyers and brochures are handed out to everyone. Salespeople will go to community events looking for ways to talk up your company, make connections, and offer solutions.

Your sales team is the closest you will come to having a true partner in your business. The good ones will be just as concerned about the overall success of the business as you are. They will push like no one else to bring revenue in. They will hold your administrative teams to task if they aren't fulfilling the promises that were made during the sales cycle. Your sales team can be a huge asset to you. And when you have a high-quality sales team, it just makes everything else run better in your business.

Be absolutely diligent about the quality and integrity of your sales team. Hold them to the highest performance standards, and never accept anything less than the absolute best. Your alternative is to buy stock in antacids as you watch your business barely survive year after year.

11

Why do we have to mark everything down before we can sell it?

Because You Think Your Products Are Crap, And Your Customers Agree.

When sales start to fall, it's natural for business owners to wonder if there is a problem with their products. If they are a service business, they may start to look at their employees and see if the services are still high quality. You can start to question whether or not the market has moved on without you. It's easy to start questioning everything you do and start revamping all your products with new features.

It's also the wrong approach.

Depending on who you ask, there are a number of pricing strategies that will work. But since you asked me, there are only two—outrageously high and unbelievably low. Everyone who talks about something in the middle is just hedging their bets. But I'll even go one step further and tell you there is only one price strategy that will work for your business, and it has nothing to do with your personal preference. It is all about the product or service you have decided to sell.

It is quite simple really. If you are offering a high-end product or service that generates results and is something you truly believe in, then you need to go the high-price route. People who enjoy luxury or exclusive items have no set budget for these things. Price it so that you make a bunch of money and market it like crazy to these people. But if you are offering a low-end or very common product or service, then you are going to end up in a pricing war, and you will have to discount like everyone else just to get money in the door and product off the shelf.

The great recession from 2008–2010 taught consumers a very valuable lesson. With the economy falling, unemployment rising, and living costs like food and gas going up, disposable income nearly disappeared in middle America. With so few dollars being spent, retailers had to make a choice about how to keep going. Should they offer their items at a discount or try to wait things out? So what did retailers do? They marked everything down—a lot.

Consumers took notice. Spending increased as the prices of goods started to come down. When retailers tried to bring prices back up, consumer loyalty disintegrated. Consumers targeted the deal, and if you weren't a retailer willing to offer the deal, then you weren't going to get any of the few dollars being spent.

So discount wars began, where the clearance section was the most popular area of many stores. Consumers started focusing more on what they were saving rather than what they were spending. As the economy recovered, retailers realized they were in for a difficult fight. Consumers had spent two years evaluating products and decided the discounted prices were the right value. They weren't ready to pay more.

Retailers knew from the beginning that discounting was going to be short term, and in order to stay profitable the prices were going to have to come back up. In 2011 and 2012, you started to see retailers trying out new strategies to counteract this value imbalance. JC Penny tried to put together an "everyday low price" strategy. What did they find? Even if the prices are the same, consumers would rather buy when they see 40 percent off.

So why do you have to discount? Because your customers don't think your products are worth what you are charging for them. Now it's up to you to decide your strategy. Are your products so good that their value is misunderstood? Do you need to spend time and money convincing the world your prices are fair? Or should you mark things up a bit so you can show your amazing discount offer and really get the original price you wanted? Of course, the real answer is creating a solution that no one else offers.

Too often businesses forget what it is they are really providing to their customers. Do you really think I buy a toothbrush because I want a toothbrush? Hell no! I buy a toothbrush so my teeth don't rot and fall out of my head. I buy a toothbrush so my dentist doesn't bring out the long needle and the drill. But most importantly, I buy a toothbrush because I know I'll never get another kiss from my wife if I don't!

If you want to stop discounting, then you need to understand what you are truly selling to your customers. You don't sell products or services. This isn't semantics, and it isn't consultant speak. Don't dismiss this simply because it sounds like a cliché. You sell solutions to problems. I've seen enough eye rolls to know this is not what most business owners want to hear or think about. It's the blowhard classroom stuff that doesn't mean much out in the real world. It's the kind of thing people say when they haven't spent a lifetime running a business.

Go ahead and keep thinking that. I'll roll my eyes and tell you that is the attitude keeping you from growing your business. When you can accept the fact you are selling a solution to a problem, everything about your business gets easier.

It's easier to talk to your market when you know what it is you really do. It's easier to be creative with your products and services. It's easier to sell when you are offering a solution. It's easier to set a vision for your company when you know who you are trying to serve. It's easier to define success when you understand the change you are making in your market and the lives of those who need your products.

Imagine the power you would have in your business if your entire focus was on solving a single problem. Not providing a specific product, but a solution to a problem. The iPod was a solution to a problem most people didn't even know they had. Music was just going into a digital format. Consumers were tired of buying CDs just to find that there were only one or two songs they really wanted. File-sharing sites were moving individual songs all around the Internet.

CD burners started coming standard on computers, so users would simply download their songs, burn them to a CD, and then play them in their cars. But what Apple did was truly amazing. They realized the advantage of the digital format of songs. By compressing them and putting them on a small hard drive, people would have access to their digital music on the go.

It exploded, and record stores everywhere closed.

Why? Because the music industry and stores that sold those albums thought they sold albums. They didn't. They sold music. Well that's not entirely right. They sold a lot of bad music bundled up with a little bit of good music. Apple saw the problem and created a solution. Consumers wanted the good music without all the crap that was bundled around it. They also wanted their music to be portable. Just like a CD, they wanted to be able to play the music they bought digitally anywhere. And have you ever seen a clearance sale on Apple products? Me neither.

Sell solutions, not products.

Watch your market. Who else is creating solutions for your customers? If your sales fall, are you still solving the problem? Has the problem shifted? Has your solution become obsolete?

According to the latest census research, only about 10 percent of small businesses in the United States provide products exclusively. There are 27 percent that provide only services, leaving about two-thirds of the small businesses in the US providing some combination of products and services. Financial planners always talk about how diversity is important in every investment portfolio. I can tell you right now that you need diversity in your business offerings, too.

Providing a professional service is probably the easiest way to start a business. You don't have any inventory to worry about. Your startup capital needs are minimal. The services can be performed on site, which means you don't need a lot of retail space. And since you are probably the service provider, your profit margin is going to be very high for each hour you bill out. But there are drawbacks to it as well. The service you provide must be in demand, and you need to be amazing at it. Because you aren't providing anything customers can appreciate with their five senses, it can be difficult to get them to emotionally connect to what you are selling.

Products, on the other hand, are right there to be seen and held. They already have intrinsic value just by having been created. But a business that is focused on products is expensive to get started. You need to handle your inventory. You need a place to showcase your products. Your cash flow is tied up in products until they are sold. Then there's that other problem, you know, Wal-Mart.

Big chain stores are driving prices so low that most small businesses simply can't compete. Unless you have found a specialty retail niche, you will constantly be competing on price with the Wal-Marts of the world, and your profits will shrivel into nothing.

Products and services have a great way of complementing each other inside small businesses. The only way to generate true wealth in your business is to develop the right product/service mix. One of my first jobs was working for a bike and ski shop. We sold some high-end equipment, but the most profitable thing we did was tune-ups on mountain bikes. It took us about fifteen to twenty minutes per bike, and we could charge anywhere from fifty to a hundred dollars for the service.

But taking a service company and adding products can be a little trickier. It takes a measure of creativity to be able to look at the services you perform and find a matching product to go with them. But this is where successful service companies will differentiate themselves from the pack. We are rapidly approaching the point in time where the need for our traditional service professionals will disappear. One example of an industry at risk is the certified public accountant.

At one point in time while I was completing my degree, I had thoughts of becoming a CPA. It seemed like a great job, busy as hell for four months and then pretty laid back for the rest of the year. While I was working on my degree, Enron collapsed. Arthur Andersen failed. The Flat Tax was gaining traction, and the future of CPAs everywhere seemed like it was slipping away. But time passed, and we all moved on.

I started working for a CPA firm my last semester of school. It was quite the eye-opening experience to me. Even though this was a large firm, the first two or three meetings I attended were about how to justify their fees. There was a lot of attention paid to H&R Block and how they handled their business. Smaller tax providers were either acquired or their client base was harvested in order to help eliminate price competition. Then the tax season started, and it was nothing like I expected. Busy as hell isn't even close to how I would describe what those months were like. Later I found out that almost 80 percent of the firm's revenue was generated in those three months of tax season.

So why do I think CPA's are in trouble now? Because of what I call the "productization of services." The vast majority of consumers think about their taxes in late January when they are reminded that a W-2 is on the way. They go out and shop for a solution and see that they can pay a CPA three hundred dollars, or they can go online and do it themselves for ten bucks. CPAs have been going up against this type of competition for years, and they could always point to their experience and their personal attention as differentiating factors. What has happened now, though, is that software companies are utilizing CPAs for support roles. They have developed the software to electronically import tax documents. They have created smart wizards to help walk people through the entire process of completing their taxes. In short, the software has caught up to and in many ways (price) surpassed the benefits of a CPA.

This is the perfect example of productization of services. As tax revenue dwindles, CPAs will have to look at other aspects of their business to generate revenue. There are many different areas where CPAs can excel, but how many will have the energy to change their focus mid-career? If you are a strictly service-oriented business, you should take a look around and see if there is a software solution that is ready to take your place.

The product or service you currently provide obviously solves an important problem. It's why people are buying it from you. But for how long is this problem going to exist? What other options do your customers have?

When it comes to the product/service mix, one of the biggest problems business owners run into is walking away from opportunity because it doesn't fit their core. If you have the chance to solve the problems of your customers, you better jump on it. Don't limit yourself and your business because you think it is outside of your original business idea. Your business is not your products and services. You are in business to solve problems. The products and services you sell are the methods you use to solve those problems.

We have moved into the age of transformation. Customers are no longer looking to buy products and services. They are much too cynical for that. They are looking for the transformation your product offers. Think about a gym membership. Do you think people are paying money to lift weights or to run on a treadmill? Hell no! They are paying for the twenty pounds they want to lose or the six-pack abs they want to show off at the beach. It's the transformation your product offers that people buy, so make sure you aren't just solving a problem—you need to provide a change in your customer's lives!

12

Why can't we ever hire anyone good?

Because Your Hiring Process Is Broken.

Whatever made you think your business would be better with employees? Was it the fact you had more work than you could get done by yourself, or were you just lonely and needed someone you could talk to?

By the way many business owners hire their first few employees, you would think their goal was to have a friend in the office more than a productive team. Hey, I get it, you are going to be spending a lot of time with these people so they have to match your personality. But if you are complaining about the quality of your employees and all you have are people you get along with, then maybe hiring a couple personality duds who are highly effective workers might be a good change of pace.

Here's something your HR department doesn't want you to know: according to the 2007 Management Action Programs (MAP) Quarterly CEO Survey conducted by Vantage Research, 32 percent of the CEOs surveyed report that up to 50 percent of their *new* employees haven't been meeting expectations over the past two years. In other words, these companies spent thousands of dollars on hiring and training when a flip of the coin would have been just as good of a predictor of the future success of these new employees. Think how much money you could save by replacing your HR department with the flip of a quarter or a Magic 8 Ball!

Hiring is not an exact science. It's time consuming and kills productivity. Training takes too long, and hiring someone who doesn't fit in with the other existing employees just creates more problems than it is worth. Plus there's that other little issue everyone seems to know ahead of time but we always seem surprised when it happens to us: people lie. They lie on their resume. They lie in their interviews. They exaggerate the positives, and minimize the negatives: if someone is unemployed, it's because his last boss didn't think he was valuable enough to keep. That should be a red flag. If she is currently employed and looking for a new job, is it because she has no loyalty or does she just resent working for the people who are currently giving her a job? Another red flag. Everyone who is job hunting has a prepared answer for why he or she is looking. But I've found it really doesn't matter.

Finding out their greatest strength and biggest weakness? Nah, waste of time. Tell me a time you were challenged? Yawn. I once did an interview where I asked the candidate about his favorite movie and the types of books he liked to read. I learned more about him with those questions than anything else I asked in the interview. My suggestion for interviewing is to ditch the common questions and find ways to get the candidate to talk—about himself (or herself), the weather, the industry, their experiences, school, you know, whatever you can. Get candidates out of their comfort zone and see how they respond. It's a much more honest interview.

But if you really want to improve your odds of getting a great employee, you need to forget any thoughts you might have had that better interviewing will give you better employees. Companies that know how to train and develop their staff have the best employees—no exceptions. It has nothing to do with the hiring process and everything to do with the ninety days after you hired your employee.

Building a team can be a daunting task. What I suggest is that you clearly identify the needs of your organization before you hire anyone. Make sure the position you are hiring for is well defined with a clear purpose or outcome you are expecting from the person who will fill this opening. Be able to explain the daily duties and the major projects this person will work on. Don't hire someone with the attitude that you'll find something for them to do. This is a quick way to be overstaffed, waste money, and lower productivity.

I worked with a business owner who ended up hiring three people to fill one opening. During the interview process, he knew he had three very talented, highly qualified people. He didn't want to miss out on the chance to add them all to his team. Rather than choosing one, he hired all three believing he could find a place for all of them. Instead, there wasn't enough work to go around, and the three of them ended up leaving.

Always get the best person for the job. Hire based on past performance and results. Don't hire based on potential—especially when you are just starting out. You don't have the resources to take chances on a person reaching his or her potential. Build urgency and accountability with your staff by bringing in top talent every time you hire.

Once you hire a person, review his performance carefully early on. Compare his performance to the qualifications he used to get the job. Do they match up? This is the quickest test I have found to evaluate the effectiveness of the hiring process. If you get employees who have performances that match their resumes, then you should feel good about the process you are using to evaluate candidates.

One last point on hiring—don't hold on to bad employees or bad hires. As soon as you realize an employee or new hire isn't a fit, it's time to move on. Don't try to fix the situation or the person. It sounds cold, but you are really doing your business and that person a favor. It's best to move on rather than continue to struggle.

Employee development is a major key in building a great team. Once you get the right employees, you need to think about your training program. What are you focused on when trying to bring new employees to your firm? Remember, your growth is partly based on the success of your employees so you need to make sure they have everything they need to be successful.

Employees will define their success on their own if you aren't there to provide guidance. If you train an employee that submitting her monthly reports is the most important part of the job, then guess what? That employee will define her success based on how well she submits that report. If you want to get your company growing again, you are going to need your new employees to bring new energy and new vibrancy to your culture.

When you are evaluating your employees, focus your energy on developing a culture that fits your overall growth goals. Are you looking to be number one in sales? Then you need creative, energetic people in your marketing and sales team. You need motivated service people to revolutionize your customer experiences. You need amazing people in your product-development departments, innovating new ideas and ways to create new opportunities in your market. What you do not need is people who are looking for "just a job" or people who are more focused on a task list than a culture of producing great work.

Keeping your employees focused means recognizing results. Whether the result is positive or negative, employees' actions need to be recognized. When an employee feels unappreciated, his or her effort will start to wane. If employees feel that others are getting away with bad work, their motivation will wane.

Public recognition of greatness can be inspiring to everyone if it is done right. Explain how the actions fit into the culture of the business. Recognize that the effort was important and that it was an action that everyone should try to copy. Don't praise exclusively in private, but do make sure you offer some private comments so the person feels uniquely rewarded.

When negative results pop up, you need to address them immediately. Use them as training moments for the whole team. In private talk about how the person can correct the behavior. In public, again discuss the results in terms of your company's culture. By reinforcing how it affects the company, you are taking the sting out of the issue and making it a commentary on appropriate behavior.

Training is a vital part of building a team of engaged employees. One overlooked team-building practice is a seat evaluation. In short, do you have the right people in the right positions? Now, I usually get a lot of push back on this topic. All business owners believe that they are very careful about who they hire, whom they promote, and how they find the right fit. Your role as the leader is a vital one, but it becomes even more pressing as you add members to your team. You've heard the expression that it only takes one bad apple to ruin the whole bunch, right? Well, the same applies to your employees. It only takes one bad employee to ruin the attitudes, productivity, and momentum of the whole team. How you build and maintain your team is going to have a huge impact on the success of your business.

A great tennis player can dominate the sport. Roger Federer was ranked number one for a record 237 consecutive weeks. He won sixteen grand slam titles another record. In basketball, a great player can dominate the sport statistically, but he won't be able to win championships without some help—think LeBron James. In football, a great player can have an impact on a game, and maybe a season, but even the best player can't completely dominate the sport without help from his teammates.

This could be the metaphor for any number of small businesses. As a solo entrepreneur, you were responsible for it all. Your success and your setbacks were the result of your own experience, ability, and effort. As your business grew, you had to make choices about the activities you were going to do and the activities you were going to need to pass on to others. Knowing that business owners who try to do it all themselves never get ahead, you pushed forward and hired your first employee. Eventually you created a small team of employees and vendors to support your business. Now your success is in some part dependent on the skills and effort of your team. As you continue to grow, your team becomes even more complex. Eventually your experience, ability, and effort will have less of an effect on your success than the effort and ability of your team.

In any sport, and we'll use football for an example here, you have very defined positions. The best organizations will put a value on each position. Some teams will value the quarterback very highly and will put a lot of resources toward getting the best of the best. Other teams may value another position more highly and be willing to take a lesser quarterback in order to afford players at these other positions. In the end, though, these teams have to identify all the positions that need to be filled and how important those positions are to their success.

How often do you look at your company the same way? Are you identifying all of the potential positions that need to be filled at your company? Don't just think of departments like marketing, sales, and accounting. Think of the individual positions that are needed. Do you need someone to run payroll, accounts payable, accounts receivable, and a controller in your accounting department? Sure, you need all of those roles filled, but do you need one person for each role? How important is each position? Do you need to invest more in a controller than, say, a position in your marketing department? These are the questions and evaluations that you need to do in order to start building the right team.

In many organizations, positions are created in response to the skills and talents of employees. For example, you hired Amy to be one of your customer-service representatives. Amy has a talent for talking with your customers and has received several glowing recommendations. After a year or two, it becomes clear that Amy is getting bored with her job. Because she is such a good employee, you decide it would be best to find a "better" job for her to fill. With nothing really open in the company, a new title is created to give Amy some recognition and new responsibilities.

This is a common practice in small businesses. The problem is that if Amy wasn't already with the company, you wouldn't have hired her to fill that role. The role wasn't entirely necessary. It was a way to appease your employee without really adding any benefit to the team. In the end, Amy will get bored again, and the rest of the team will resent her position and start expecting similar chances for themselves.

It all goes back to that initial analysis and deciding what positions you need to fill in your company. This is a process that you will need to revisit often so you will get better at it with practice. You need to develop a system, though, of how you identify the needs in your organization.

Now, granted, that process is a lot easier when you don't already have employees. But once you have identified the roles your organization needs and the value of the role to your overall success, you will start evaluating the fit of each employee. The value you assign to each position is very critical in this process. Many times I have heard business owners talk about a person as "the best fit we have" for a position. Just because someone is the best fit you currently have, it doesn't mean he or she is the best person to fill that position.

When I evaluate a team, I look at the high-value positions first. Let's not confuse high value with high paying. In my opinion, the positions that have the most influence on the cash flow of the company are the ones that should be high value. After that, I rank the positions that have the most influence on other employees. In other words, sales and accounting first, then management. After that it starts to depend on the industry. Other business owners rank positions differently, and you will need to find what works for you.

Once you've identified your high-value positions, find the absolute best person you can to fill those roles. Remember, you have identified these positions as having the most effect on your business's success, so invest heavily and get the best talent you can. Then keep working your way down the value chain.

When you are looking for the best fit, you should be evaluating on a structured criteria. The three main questions I ask in my evaluation are:

- Does this person understand the job?
- Does this person have genuine enthusiasm for the work this job requires?
- Does this person have the ability to do the work?

So the first question is whether the person understands the job. This is especially relevant in positions that are fairly technical or require some extended knowledge. The first test is whether this person can discuss the ins and outs of the job and how it fits into the overall business plan. Look at the education and training of this person; does it match the requirements of this job? You want to make sure this person has a reasonable chance at being successful in this position.

The second question is about the attitude this person displays. An unhappy employee is going to be unhappy no matter what you do with his or her position. So is this a person who really enjoys the work he or she is doing or who is just going through the motions? You want to find people who are actively looking for ways to improve the performance of the company. This only comes from people who truly enjoy the work they are doing. These people require little managing and even less motivation. You can set them in the right direction and watch them go! Build a team full of these people, and you will be moving faster than you ever thought possible.

Finally, we need to evaluate the person's ability. Is this position going to be challenging without being overwhelming to this person? Having someone in a position that is beneath his or her abilities is a fast track to boredom which leads to unhappiness. The job needs to be challenging to keep the employee's interest. You also need to evaluate whether or not this person has developed the skills that are required for the job. This is certainly the more technical analysis that you will do with each seat.

There are other concerns that will need to be met, but these three are the big ones. At the very least you can use these three criteria as a way to start the process. I guarantee if one of your employees fails one of these three tests, he or she will never be the right fit for that position, and that will continue to hurt your performance. If several people meet all three of these criteria, then you can use whatever system you want to narrow the field to the one person who fits the role the best.

Building the right team is an ongoing process, and it will impact the performance of your company. A seat analysis gives you the best system to make sure all of your roles are being filled with the right people. Shift your thoughts about how to bring on new employees. Thinking about it as just hiring keeps you in search of superstars and makes it easier for people to lie to you in their interviews. You get wrapped up in their potential and fail to see the tell tale signs of a problem child.

Instead, think about it as the process of building a team. You need to hire people who fit the team and fill the role you have designed. Complaining about not being able to hire good people is more about your training and team-building skills than it is your interviewing and recruitment process. Put your efforts where they belong, and the quality of your staff will continually rise.

13

Why are we wasting time on projects that have nothing to do with our business?

Because You Haven't Set A Vision For Your Business.

have spent a good portion of my life around teachers. Anyone who is willing to share what they know with others should be cherished. But I have a soft spot for schoolteachers because the task they have chosen to take on is more than most of us could ever endure. Keeping the attention of a classroom full of kids is hard enough on a normal school day, but it can be damn near impossible for them to keep it as summer vacation approaches.

Imagine the challenge that high-school teachers have in keeping graduating seniors focused. My senior English teacher was a master at it. He showed up to school every day in flannel shirts and work boots. He had long hair that looked like a comb had never touched it and a full-on lumberjack beard. Whether this was truly him or a part he played, I don't know for sure. What I do know is that I never saw him out of character. And what a character! There was a little crazy in him for sure, and he'd act out just enough to keep us all on edge. Whether it was an off-the-wall story, his obsession with killing yellow jackets with just a finger, or some of the weirdest assignments ever, we all made sure to show up every day to see what he had in store for us.

What he managed to do was fulfill his vision without us even knowing it was all an act. He knew his audience. He knew we were more likely to skip class and slack off in that last year of high school. As seniors we would all look for the easy route and for our teachers to make exceptions for us. But his vision was to have a class that people wanted to come to. He didn't have any control over the content of the course, so he created a character that got the students talking. He created fear in students who didn't take his class, wonder in those that did. Twenty-plus years later I can barely remember the names of most of the kids I went to school with, but I remember that class.

One of the assignments he gave us that year was to write a journal. In the journal, we were to do two things: every day we had to record what we had accomplished since the last entry, and at the end of the year we had to make a prediction of what we would be doing ten years in the future. It was supposed to be a look at our whole life, so not just what our job would be but also our social circles, our relationships, our day-to-day activities, you know, everything. Talk about a stretch of the imagination. We were eighteen and clueless. No one cared about what his or her life was going to be like that far ahead, but we tried anyway because no one was quite sure what would happen if we didn't.

I bring this up because I recently found that journal and started reading it again. Just the advancements in technology can make some of the predictions seem quite silly, and I can say my life is almost nothing like the one I predicted for myself. But there are some big ideas that I was able to predict. I am married, I have a son, and I own my business.

However, I do not live in Hawaii, I didn't play professional football (not that I played high-school football either—not sure how I planned to make that work), and a hundred other predictions didn't come true. As hard as the process was to predict my life in high school, many entrepreneurs find it equally difficult to predict the success and structure of their own business.

As an entrepreneur, you have the unwavering belief that your product or service is going to change the world. It can feel like there is no way you can fail. So why is it that only a small number of entrepreneurs are absolutely right and are able to find immediate and long-term success? The vast majority of small businesses fails in fewer than five years.

Too often the wrong people decide to start a business. They get told that they have a real talent for something and should do it full time. Maybe they were laid off and are looking to start a business rather than going to work for someone else. It could be that they have such a strong belief in their dream that they just won't be satisfied until they try it on their own. But being good at something or believing in something isn't enough to start, maintain, and grow a business. With a strong vision about what you want to do, it's easy to stay focused. But if you aren't sure what your business is supposed to be, or do, it is easy to get distracted. And if you are distracted, you can pretty much bet your employees are going to be distracted, too!

Distractions are a part of business. There is always some task or event that can come up that keeps you from getting your work done. You could end up in a sales meeting rather than finishing up the work for one of your existing clients. You could have to deal with a bookkeeping error or a problem at the bank rather than working with your customer-service team. These distractions are normal and frequent. You are going to have to work these out on your own.

But there is another type of distraction that is even more devastating to businesses. I call it the "shiny red toy" distraction. It's when you can't shut down the creative part of your mind. You see opportunities everywhere, and you want to pursue them all. Rather than building on the processes, products, and services that will grow your business, you want to find the next greatest thing. And that's OK for you, if your business can handle its work without you. But if you are taking your business with you on this journey, then you are going to be in trouble.

Your business must have a clear direction. You can go down as many rabbit holes as you want, but your business must have a unique purpose. As a leader, you need to create and communicate your vision for the company. This may sound rather simple, but it is the first step to a larger plan. Your business has probably created a mission or vision statement in the past. It may even be engraved on a plaque and hanging in the lobby of your office. If it is like most mission statements, it has a lot of fluff and no substance. Take a look at this example from a construction company:

We are a leader in providing value-added construction services to our customers by creating a successful partnership with them throughout the construction process. Our pledge is to establish lasting relationships with our customers by exceeding their expectations and gaining their trust through exceptional performance by every member of the construction team and to provide our employees with an honest and helpful working environment, where every employee individually and collectively can dedicate themselves to providing our customers with exceptional workmanship, extraordinary service, and professional integrity.

Why couldn't they just say, "We make the best damn buildings in the world"? It would save on the engraving costs!

More importantly, though, it boils the message down to the most important part of the company. It is a construction company. It builds things. Its mission is to build the best possible buildings it can. Why talk about successful partnerships and exceeding customers' expectations when you can drill it down to being the best?

As the leader of your organization, you need to develop that very short and powerful mission statement. You know what your business will do. It doesn't have to be on a plaque, and it doesn't have to be inspirational. But it does need to be the guiding principle for your business.

Now there is a school of thought out there that says a mission or vision statement should cover the culture of the business and the values it believes in. You have to choose how you want to go here. My feeling is that values and culture are defined by the actions of our leaders and not by their words. If you live your values and run your business based on your values, you won't need them engraved on a plaque. It's your choice.

So take a look at your mission statement and see if it really identifies what it is your company does. Here is the test: take your mission statement to a school and see how many ten-year-olds can tell you what your business does based on your mission statement.

The best mission statements are simple and provide direction to everyone in the company. "We make the best damn buildings in the world." If I worked in the purchasing department and I had to make a tough choice about my suppliers, I would know that the quality of the materials is the most important factor. If I worked as a project manager, I would know that delaying the project to fix a section that doesn't meet our standards is more important than finishing on time. Look at the first mission statement. How do you think the employees in those situations would respond if that mess was their guiding principle?

The fact is, they wouldn't use it as a guide. Mission statements that are that big and fluffy are rarely ever made into an important part of the company. So create a clear vision for what your company does by developing a strong mission statement.

Some companies decide to have both a mission statement and a vision statement. The mission statement talks about what you do, and the vision statement talks about what the company will be in five or ten years. If you choose to have the vision statement, be very specific about what your company will achieve. Use very precise words in your description. Instead of "We will be the largest" say "We will have annual revenues of."

When you are creating your mission statement, try to think back to the reasons you started your business. Allow yourself to think big. Try to develop a very clear message that you want to share with every employee, customer, and supplier in your business. This doesn't have to be a profound statement by any means, but it should be able to identify the path your business will take in the future.

The best mission statements have strong active verbs in them. "We will create the best product" is better than "We will be known for creating the best products." The first statement has fewer words and defines a clear path. The second statement, even though it sounds the same, actually has more doubt behind it. Known by who? Did we create these products in the past? What are we doing now? It is just a weaker statement.

Is there an ideal or principle that you are passionate about? Some entrepreneurs are looking to make a social statement with their products. Others would like to bring about changes in different areas such as medicine or poverty. Perhaps there is a charity or a cause that you would like to bring awareness to. All of these ideals appeal to the better parts of our humanity. What does your business appeal to?

When a business has a mission and a vision that are based on the product or service of the company, it is easy for everyone to understand the priorities. But if you really want to build momentum, you need to communicate to everyone a higher purpose for their work. You need to create a vision that appeals to their better selves.

Think about the idea of bringing awareness to breast cancer. You, personally—not your company, you—could volunteer at a breast-cancer event. You could put articles about breast cancer in your newsletter. You could host screening clinics or offer to have on-site mammograms for your female employees and the wives of your male employees. Taking these actions changes you from a person who just speaks about big vision into a person of action. Now those around you, employees and customers, will see you and your company as more than just a business. You now have a business with a purpose. And instead of seeing a business owner, they will see a leader who is stepping out in front of the business and making commitments to a higher ideal.

Having a clearly defined purpose for your business is more than just putting together a few words. It can be just as useful for future planning as a budget, marketing plan, or financial analysis. It can be the measuring stick for every new project, product, or service your business is looking at. "Does this fit with our mission?" If you have a team that gets distracted easily, then this question is going to be the most important one you can ask.

And if you do decide to follow a passion for a new shiny red toy, set up another business. Don't try to make it fit where it doesn't belong.

14

Why are all the good ideas already taken?

Because You Aren't Spending Any Time Or Money In Research And Development.

"Build a better mousetrap and the world will beat a path to your door." I can remember this as a true business lesson when I was still in grade school. "Invention is 1 percent inspiration and 99 percent perspiration." This is another one of those lessons on creativity that seems to stay at the front of everyone's mind. Combined, they tell the story of how innovation has been used in the past.

The innovative process used to involve a capable person dreaming up some new way to serve a purpose or solve a problem for all of humankind. By creating this new product, his dreams of fame and fortune would be realized. So for generations, people have been inspired to try and create something unique that people would buy.

Most of them failed. In fact, even the most successful inventors failed more often than they succeeded. They were just remembered for their great products and ideas. And while a small few reached fame and fortune, most inventors lived in obscurity with little to show for their ideas and their work.

When asked how they were successful, the great inventors talked about an amazing work ethic to see things to the end. The idea of invention became more about the hard work and less about the revolutionary idea. So even though creative ideas are still out there, the hard work and tiny, almost invisible success rate has turned people from invention.

Instead of creators, we have developed a population of users and copiers. Nothing original is coming out of our creative people anymore. Just look at the movie industry. How many movies coming out now are remakes of something that was done decades ago? Where did all of our original stories go?

Creativity stopped being about solving problems and started being about artistic achievement. In fact, solving problems is no longer a creative process with most companies. Most managers look for a minimum amount of effort to address the symptoms that their customer base is complaining about. It's the businesses that are willing to bring creative solutions to the actual problems that will continue to grow in this new economy.

I've talked to several people who have great ideas, but when it comes to monetizing the idea they get cold feet. They believe someone else must have already thought about it, or that it would be too hard or cost too much money to build a business around it. The ideas wither and die on the vines, and the belief that innovation, creativity, and invention is too hard for normal people continues to live on.

Look around. Times have changed. The old ways of thinking about invention need to be put to rest. Technology has changed dramatically. Think about the music industry—from vinyl to eight-tracks to cassettes to CDs to file sharing to digital downloads, and on to the next thing. Each advancement came more quickly than the previous one.

We are living in a time when raw materials are cheap and labor can be found anywhere. Businesses are no longer restricted to a geographical location. You can have your corporate office in the basement of your home in Minnesota, your shipping company in Nebraska, your products created in Asia, your customer-service team in West Virginia, and your sales and marketing teams scattered throughout the world. The infrastructure for business is better now than it has ever been if you plan on reaching a global market.

So what does that have to do with invention? Well, it really changes the models that we have held on to for so long. It is now too easy to implement an idea. Which means invention really is 99 percent inspiration and only about 1 percent perspiration. The problem we all face as business owners is that new ideas are becoming very, very rare.

Innovation has become one of the hallmarks of growing businesses. Technology is usually the first industry to come to mind when talking about innovation. Look at the new ideas that are coming out. You have smart phones, tablets, and touch-screen computers as some of the newest innovations right now. But if you look at it, none of those are original ideas. They are just different methods of utilizing a touch screen to perform computing functions that have been around for decades.

If that is true, then why is the technology industry the go-to "innovative" trendsetter? Because that is the new model of invention. Most of the original ideas in this world have been used up. Now we are looking for the best ways to utilize these ideas. How we identify a solution that works in one industry and apply it to our situation is the new innovative business model.

But we need to pause for a second and really look at the idea that most new ideas coming out aren't original. What does this mean, and what does it mean for your business? I have worked with a lot of smart people who give up on their innovative ideas too quickly. It is an unfortunate truth that many great businesses are dying before they ever get a chance to see the light of day. Why won't they see it through to the end?

For the same reason you probably are not building innovative ideas for your business. Because everyone is still looking for that one product or contraption that no one else has thought of. How many product or service ideas do you think have been dismissed because they weren't original or because someone else was doing the same thing?

That is the old way of invention, and we need to move into this new generation of thought leaders. If you see your business as providing a single product or a single service, you will have a hard time growing your wealth. Thinking of your business as a collection of assets that provide you revenue will help you build a strong and thriving revenue stream.

Creative solutions by their nature are very personal. To get the most creative energy out of your organization, you will need to create a culture that celebrates what it means to innovate. Very few people will have the internal strength to put their thoughts and emotions into the process if they feel they will be ridiculed or unappreciated.

What is the culture like at your office now? Most business owners either don't care or falsely believe that it is better than it really is. It's not an overconfidence thing; it's just that most business owners know what they think and how they feel about the business. The thought that employees have a different feeling doesn't usually enter the equation. You can answer this pretty easily by walking around and asking various employees for their best ideas on how to improve the company. The answers you get will tell you a lot about the culture of your organization from the point of view of your employees.

I would really recommend you take this step before making any of the changes I outline going forward. I especially recommend you take this step if you are thinking to yourself right now that you already know the answer!

Simply ask your employees, "What ideas do you have that would help our company become a leader in our market?" Don't focus on the quality of the ideas. Listen to hear if your employees really believe their ideas are valued or that they have some impact on the direction of the company. If your employees hesitate to offer any ideas, then you may have a culture that discourages creative thought.

You need to make fostering creativity and innovation in your organization a priority. Your business is a result of the passions you felt as an entrepreneur. Remember, creativity is a very personal experience, and not everyone is creative in the same way. Try to match creative projects to the people who are best suited for them. It doesn't make sense to have a talented artist trying to develop a new operational process. Put that person to work on a new marketing campaign. Exploring their passions will turn normal employees into creative thinkers and will keep them heavily invested in the success of the projects.

Create support systems in the organization to help your employees generate creative solutions. Many times, employees will have an idea and not share it because they aren't exactly sure how they would implement the idea. Have a system in place where the employee can share the idea and get help in the development phase. One way that I have seen this work is having an idea or project sponsored by someone in management. It is not the manager's responsibility to take the lead on the project, but he or she is responsible for answering questions and reporting on the progress of the idea. This way there is a mentorship relationship with the employees who are working on the project.

When you start working with your team, remember to keep the focus on creativity and creating assets. I cannot stress this enough to you. You will have employees who are looking for creative ways to recycle paper in the office, and while it's great for the environment and may mix well with your corporate vision, is it ever going to generate recurring revenue? Make it clear from the very beginning that no idea will be turned away, but that the ideas that are going to be pursued heavily are the ones that will generate new revenue for the company.

Start small. Continue to work within your defined core, and try to add a small, new revenue stream. I know of an insurance agent who was able to generate additional revenue by selling a small software program to his clients. He didn't even have to create the program. He acted as a reseller and collected a commission on each disk sold. It wasn't a lot of money, but it added recurring revenue and required little action on his part.

Early on it can be tough to get your momentum moving forward. For each successful idea, you will probably end up with several failed plans. How you handle those failures will determine whether you are building forward momentum or just standing still. Make sure that each time a project fails to meet its goals, you have some form of review process.

Building a business through innovation is the foundation for my friends Tom and David MacKenzie and their business, Texting Dots. Imagine trying to start a business in an industry that changes technology as quickly as the smart phone. Tom and David's story starts like most product-based businesses—they identified a need and created a solution.

Tom was watching his kids one afternoon and saw how quickly they were texting and advancing through the screens of their smart phones. He had never had much luck with these phones, and even though he tried many times to hit the buttons, his fingers were just too big. Texting was near impossible, as it took him too long, and halfway through he'd hit the wrong button and have to start over. His frustration led him on a search.

What he found in the market was a real lack of products that were designed to help people hit the keys on a phone more accurately. He had already decided he wasn't going to upgrade his phone to one of the smart phones until he had a better solution for how to use it. He had seen others use a pen to tap out texts on the little keyboards, but he wanted something better.

On a routine trip to the hardware store, he stopped in the kitchen department and looked at the cabinets. What caught his eye were the little stoppers on the back of the cabinets. Thinking about his texting problem, he bought a few of these stoppers and took them home. With a knife, he cut a small circle out of the center of one of these stoppers and peeled off the paper on the back to expose the adhesive. After sticking it on his finger, he tried texting again. He could hit the right keys, and Texting Dots was born.

Tom contacted his brother, David, and they talked extensively about how they could make these dots work. David had the connections needed to acquire materials and adhesives so they could start producing these Texting Dots. At first it was pretty easy; they developed a dot that would stick easily to the finger and then could be discarded when the person was done texting.

Now these dots are moving past the cell phone market and heading into everyday situations. The MacKenzie brothers see dots as the perfect solution for touch screens everywhere. Texting Dots are a sanitary solution for things like the airport check-in kiosks, self-check-out lines at the grocery store, or even ATMs. Texting Dots will always be the solution that was created to help people text better, but now the product is going to be visible in more industries.

Everyone has his or her own process for being creative, and it is important to develop it into something that can be repeated over and over. As I mentioned before, we are almost out of original ideas. Most everything that we come up with now is created from the building blocks of existing ideas—either in our current market or in other markets that have related problems.

Creating a new idea takes a lot of work, but it can be made easier if we are willing to accept that the solution has already been created. An artist can look at a blank canvas and already see the painting that belongs on it. A sculptor will look at a block of marble or stone and see the design that is hidden inside. For the sculptor the rock is the problem and she simply needs to remove the parts that are hiding the solution waiting inside. We are going to take the same process and apply it to creating your new assets.

When you walk into a creative process, you have to go in with the belief that the solution has already been created. Your job is to find the solution and apply it to your problem. This is a tough transition for people who consider themselves creative to accept. But until your team is willing to accept that mind shift, they will always have problems generating new assets for your company.

I have a five-step process to create new solutions:

- Evaluate
- Scan
- Adopt
- Test
- Implement

The first step is to evaluate your situation. What problem are you trying to solve, or what asset are you trying to create? This process should be a very in-depth review of what your organization is currently doing and any obstacles or potential roadblocks that may prevent a solution from working. Until you know where you are starting, you won't be able to create the right solution. Make sure you are very specific about the idea you are evaluating. Don't let the idea get so big that it never has a chance to be successful. Solving world hunger might be out of your reach, but working to feed the homeless in your city may be more manageable.

Next you need to scan the marketplace for solutions or assets that are already in place. If you are looking for a new revenue stream, look for a product that you can add to your sales mix. Don't try to create one on your own; find a product that you can resell for a commission. Other businesses or industries will have similar problems to those that you face. Look at their solutions before you try to create something on your own. Pull down as much information as you can about what already exists.

This next step might be the most controversial because it can feel like plagiarism. You are going to adopt the solution or asset that you found in the previous step. I'm not saying that you make a direct copy of someone else's marketing material. That would be an infringement on their rights. What I am saying is after you have found how others have solved the same problem, find how you can apply that same solution to your issues. You may not find an exact match of solution to problem, so this is where creativity sets in. Find a way to make the process or asset work within your company.

Once you have developed your idea, using the solutions and assets that are currently in the marketplace, you need to put it through a strict testing program. Everything looks and sounds better in the planning stage. When it comes time to actually put the program in place, it starts to fall apart. Make sure that you test the solution to see that it will work. Even more important than that, at this stage you need to go back to your "evaluate" stage and look at the problem you identified. Does the solution you developed sufficiently solve that problem? If the idea doesn't pass this testing phase, go back to step two and look for additional resources that can help solidify the idea.

The final step is where the rubber hits the road. It's time to implement your new solution. This may sound like the easy part, but most plans are left to die on the planning desk. Until you have a solid process for making sure your plan becomes an intimate part of your organization, all that hard work to create a solution will be wasted. Once implemented, review the asset or the solution regularly to be sure it is working as intended.

There you go, a quick, five-step program to get your creative teams started. You can make your innovative systems and creative teams as complex as you want, but I have found that the simpler the solution the more likely it is to be successful.

To get you started, here are some action items you can start today:

- Ask your employees for feedback about how to grow your business.
- Review your notes and look for fresh ideas that you haven't explored fully.
- Begin talking with other business owners in your network about the successes they have had in creating new ideas and products in their business. (Be willing to share your own successes as well.)
- Contact some of your repeat customers and ask for their feedback about new services or products they would like you to offer.

Look to the thought leaders in your industry. Industry conferences and trade shows always like to bring in guest speakers. Usually they try to find people who have a unique perspective on the market. Listen to their speeches, but then seek them out online or after the conference. Subscribe to their newsletters. Read any books they may have written. These people are a wealth of information. Their perspective on your market could be exactly what you need to recognize new opportunities.

You are probably already paying attention to your competitors, but if not, now is the time to start. Pay attention to any press releases they may have. Look at how they are marketing themselves. You have spent a great deal of time and money differentiating yourself from the competition. It would be naïve to think they haven't been doing the same thing. Can you spot what they are doing to differentiate themselves? Are they adding new services? Have they started selling a new product? Getting a good understanding of what your competition is doing, and why they are doing it, will help you see patterns in your market.

Have you noticed how much overlap there is between different industries and markets? Cell phones now play music and videos, update Web sites, and have navigation tools. They aren't just limited to making phone calls. How many different types of companies provide similar services in your market? Learn what these other companies are doing. What problems do they have? What are their strengths and weaknesses? Where are they putting their investment dollars? All of these are clues to tell you which way the market may be going.

Like I said before, you also need to understand your customers. Take the time to have genuine conversations with them. Listen more than you talk. Ask them to make predictions about your market and their future needs. What solutions will they be looking for in six months, twelve months, and five years from now? What hurdles or problems are they facing now? Working with all aspects of your market, you will start to see trends developing. If you have a deep understanding, you may even be able to see potential partnerships that will help grow your business. When you have a better understanding, it becomes easier to anticipate the needs of your market.

Encourage your employees to look for problems to solve in the marketplace. Look for inefficient solutions and make them better. Turn complex products into simpler solutions. Don't limit what your business can do.

Evaluate the success of your assets on their ability to provide revenue. If they provide revenue, then you need more assets just like them. If they don't provide revenue, then it is time to build a new asset. Either way, this is where innovation becomes a huge multiplier in the growth of your business. Don't fall into the starving-artist trap where you are creating things that no one will pay money to have. The key to using innovation in your business is to create new and exciting ways for your customers to purchase goods and services from you.

15

Why is everyone telling me social media is important?

Because It Is Important—To Them.

Right or wrong, I still blame the iPhone for this.

I remember my first cell phone. That thing was five pounds and looked like a brick with a massive antennae sticking out. I carried the thing in a backpack because it was too big to fit anywhere else. It had horrible reception and was a pain in the ass. Based on those first models, I'm surprised the whole cell-phone revolution even happened.

But like everything else in technology, the hardware got smaller and the processing power got bigger, and pretty soon you had phones that were more advanced than some of the first supercomputers. And they fit in my pocket. Then came MySpace, Facebook, Twitter, and a hundred others sites that seemed to have no real purpose other than wasting time. And then the iPhone came out, and business owners around the world lost any chance ever of getting productivity out of their workforce.

I've seen people who can't type more than thirty words per minute on a keyboard that can send out twenty-five status updates and forty text messages in the blink of an eye. I've walked around call centers and seen agents on the phone talking to customers while texting on their cell phones. I've seen employees tell managers to "hold that thought" while they answered their cell phones. I feel like an eighty-year-old man complaining about these damn kids and their newfangled technology. But the truth is, the world of communication has shifted. Social media is here to stay, and it's about time we found the right place for it in business.

There is a big push to incorporate social media in all marketing strategies. I am a big proponent of using every method available, but the social media thing is getting overblown. It really feels like the tech boom and bust of the late 1990s. Everyone is focused heavily on the traffic and not really following the money.

These social sites have done a very good job of creating a game-like atmosphere inside their portals. They are tapping into our basic desires for status and community. The more time you spend inside a site, the more you realize you should be adding contacts, friends, fans, or connections. The quality of these connections drops in an effort to reach the "high score" and have the most people in your network. And like any good game, it creeps into your mind and gets you to spend more and more time working on your account.

Ever since the phenomenon started, businesses have been trying to figure out how to capitalize on social media. And for good reason, too. The sheer volume of people who are actively engaged in these types of sites is staggering. You have to take notice if there is even a chance that a social-media strategy could tap into that buying power.

But nothing is ever that simple. No matter which site you look at, two-thirds of all users are on a social media site as a way to stay connected with family and friends. They are not out there to shop, buy, or sell. The other third are out there to find new friends, communicate with others, win popularity contests, and most importantly of all, research. But don't fool yourself: no one goes to their social-media profile with the intention of shopping for goods and services.

So where does this leave business owners? Well, it generally splits them into two different camps. The first camp is the social-media believers. No matter what you tell them, they see unlimited potential with the platform. They look at the eight hundred million plus active users and think, "All I need is a half of a half of a half of a half of a percent of that to make my sales numbers go out of this world." So they go all out with paid advertisements, full-time staff members, and a flood of dollars to find those few people out there that will buy. But what they are really doing is alienating people by trying to invade what they feel is a noncommercial space.

But I have seen social media work to grow a business. This business owner took a unique tactic with her social-media presence. Rather than paying for ads, she used it as a way to promote newsworthy items. All day, every day, she was posting news articles and funny sayings that had to do with the problems her business solved. Her business was about getting all-natural, all-organic food into stores. So one day she would post an article about insecticides on produce. Another day would be about hormones given to livestock. As she educated people on the social-media sites, she was also proving the problem she solved and offering an opportunity to get more information. It was a masterful way of using social media to draw out new leads.

The second camp is the social-media naysayers. They see social media as a passing fad and a waste of time. They know people aren't buying out there, so they don't see any need to waste time, money and resources on something that simply won't give them any results. But they forget that last reason people use social media—research. If your company doesn't have a social-media presence, it's like not having a Web site. People wonder if you are a real business.

So is social media important? Yes, when it's done right. Social media gives you the opportunity to communicate with your customers. It gives you an opportunity to tell a story about your business. It gives you an outlet to build trust with your market and prospective customers. It can be very useful as a way to generate new leads. But it is not a revenue machine. It is not an untapped market of potential sales. Social media is the new public relations department.

Another business owner I worked with used social media as a tool to spread testimonials about his services. He would encourage happy customers to post their experience on his Web page or social-media site. It was a self-repeating process. As one person would post about his great experience, several other people would see the posts and make their own testimonial comments. Word spread quickly about the quality of service with a long string of happy customers eagerly telling their stories online.

In order to make social media work for your business, you need to account for these two things: permanence and virility. When e-mail was starting to go mainstream, everyone was amazed at how quickly a private message could be sent to another person. It was the privacy of a letter with the speed and convenience of the phone. But then everyone found out those messages weren't so private. The advice coming from computer experts was to not put anything in an email you wouldn't want to have printed in the newspaper.

Social media is the exact same thing only faster. Once you send something, all it takes is one person to take notice, and it starts spreading throughout the interwebs. One share goes to five hundred people, ten of those share to another five hundred each, and on and on. And of course, the more embarrassing (good or bad) the comment is, the faster and further it will travel. This is the seductive part of social media to marketers. If they could just come up with the right post, tweet, or pin, then the message could hit hundreds of thousands of people in hours or days.

It's a great strategy when the message that travels is positive and generates genuine interest in your company. But those aren't usually the messages that have that kind of reach. Negativity and scandals have more staying power in the social-media world. Just like a virus, the message will multiply, expand, and morph into something that can be very damaging to your company.

The other concern about social media is how these messages are stored. Even if you delete a message, someone somewhere still has a record of it. They can still pass it around and get the sharing process started again. So your social-media strategy needs to be well controlled, and it needs to have reasonable goals.

An overemphasis on getting a viral marketing message going could lead your team down some scary avenues where your company may get painted in a negative light. So try to hold back your marketing enthusiasm in social media.

The best strategy in the social-media world is to treat it like a customer-service tool. Use it as a way to communicate with your customers. But be warned: your customers are expecting a conversation, not a press release. They want interaction, so you will need to tailor your messages with that in mind. Respond to questions and create unique offers for those who choose to follow you. Create excitement with "Talk to the CEO" chat sessions, where customers can express themselves directly to you. Then you can control the conversation and the answers to put the best positive spin on your company in the social-media world.

While social media can be a great tool for your business, beware of the time it requires. It will drain your time and the time of your team if you let it. Before long you will need someone full time monitoring your social-media sites if you allow things to grow too fast or if you don't put limits on your social-media strategy.

Schedule specific events to answer questions, create offers, and respond to direct questions. But unless you want to create a full-time social media job on your team, don't go much farther than that.

Even with all the potential drawbacks to using social media in your business, there are some advantages. Social media can be a versatile tool in public relations. It can enhance your customer experience by providing a near-immediate way for you to communicate directly to your customers. Social media can help further your marketing plans by being an inexpensive way to promote your events and new offers. It can even help generate new leads for your sales team. Just remember to keep the proper perspective on your social-media strategy. It's not going to be the window to record-breaking profits, but it just might be the best tool for managing your public image.

16

Why are my costs going through the roof?

Because You Are Wasting Money.

J
ustify it all you want, but if your costs are climbing it's because there is
too much waste in your company. Some of the biggest arguments I've
ever been in with clients had nothing to do with strategy, marketing,
personnel, or performance. They were about the expenses of the business.

When I first got started with my business, I sought out as much advice
as I could get. I talked to professors and business coaches. I talked to
finance people at banks and investment houses. I read books and magazines, downloaded whitepapers, watched videos, and interviewed "experts."
I met with people in networking groups and finally settled in and talked to
several business owners.

Everyone said similar things: have a great product, market it well, be
active in the community, make sure you have enough cash reserves to survive the first six months, and on and on. But in all of this research, there
was one comment that stuck with me: "Watch your expenses like a hawk.
There are so many things in the business world that are out of your control, but not your expenses. You have 100 percent control over how much
you spend. Spend too much too soon, and you are out of business."

So who said it? Was it the financial planners or banks? Nope. Was it the experts or professors? Nope. Was it the business owners? I wish it were, but again no. It was a friend of mine. Someone who had never run his own business and never had any desire to do so. We were having lunch and talking about my business plan when he said those amazing words to me. Of all the things business owners deal with on a daily, weekly, and monthly basis, the only thing you are guaranteed to be able to control are your expenses.

So if you as a business owner are in control, why are your expenses climbing?

Like I said before, it's because you have allowed too much waste to enter your business. I worked for a company that was ecstatic about a 5 percent profit margin. My salary was doubled in less than six months when I showed them how implementing a few small reforms could take them from a 5 percent profit margin up to 15 percent. When I left the company, they were operating at a remarkable (for them) 22 percent profit margin, and we really only worked on the expense side of the ledger. Had we put as much effort into the revenue side of things, that profit margin could have been even larger.

But the point that has always bothered me about looking at the profit margin is how it hides the expenses. When things are good and the company is doing well, profit margin is a great report card. It is something all of your stakeholders recognize and can appreciate. But when you are struggling and trying to make changes, profit margin doesn't provide much guidance. In fact, it can confuse your strategy. Is your profit margin down because your expenses are too high or because revenue is too low? Is it better to go after more revenue or try to cut costs or maybe a little of both? Indecision becomes inaction, inaction creates more problems, more problems create anxiety, and anxiety creates rash decisions. Then you are really in a hole.

So flip profit margin around and use it as an "expense quotient." Instead of a 15 percent profit margin, you have an 85 percent expense quotient. It is the ratio between your expenses and revenue. Now you have a very clear picture of how much money you are really spending—eight-five cents out of every dollar you earn is being spent on something in the business. And now you are back in control of your expenses.

Don't underestimate the power of the expense quotient in managing your expenses. Almost every company I've ever worked for has used budget cuts as a way to save money in an effort to either improve cash flow or profit margin. Usually it ends up with a blanket statement that every department must cut a certain percentage from its budget.

Some of the more progressive business owners or financial wizards will even talk about *kaizen*, which is a concept from Deming's work in Total Quality Management. At its best, kaizen is about continuous improvement in an organization by trying to improve efficiency. At its worst, kaizen is about continuous cost reductions in an effort to get the most production with the least expense.

But in general, these blanket efforts to cut costs ultimately fail. Cutting 10 percent from every department never works. For one, some departments generally are doing a good job at holding down their costs. For another, some managers know exactly how to negotiate points so they don't have to cut costs in their department. I've never seen a sales manager who wasn't good enough to convince his superiors that cutting costs out of his sales team would only cut revenue for the year. So the back and forth plays out and the budget may get whittled down a bit, but the waste is already built in.

How often do you hear stories of managers who go on spending sprees at the end of a quarter or budget year because they were afraid if they didn't spend the money they'd lose it next year? If only it were just a story. I've seen it. Hell, I've done it.

This is how the expense quotient can make a real difference in cost cutting. Knowing the ratio of expenses to revenue gives you a snapshot on what your company is spending your money on. Now, you could take your income statement and run percentages along all of your expense items and see how they relate to revenue. Yawn. It's easy to do, provides little useful information, and undervalues the power of the expense quotient.

Instead, use it on something meaningful. On your income statement, you can figure out that payroll has a 55 percent expense quotient. But what about individual teams? What is the expense quotient for your customer-service team? And not just payroll, but all of the expenses they use—phone, Internet, software, hardware, furniture, etc. What is the true expense quotient of your sales team? Now think about projects. What was the true expense quotient of a marketing campaign or a software upgrade? What is the expense quotient of your technology?

You can use your expense quotient to analyze the timing of expenses, too. Compare the quarterly expenses of departments, projects, and systems. Do you have outrageously high expense quotients at the end of budget periods? Are there teams that are simply spending money to keep that same number in next year's budget?

See, with a little work, you can have amazing insight into how your company is spending money. This is the power of the expense quotient—it puts you back in control of every dollar your company spends. Now you have targeted information to work with. You can cut costs where they are wasteful rather than sending out a blanket order to cut the budget by 10 percent.

I know from experience that every expense is important. But what I also know is that expenses left unchecked become a burden to the profitability of every company. Rather than spending time justifying expenses or arguing about the validity of an expense with your team, put that time into implementing an expense quotient analysis. You will be amazed at how differently you view the importance of your expenses!

The most common financial mistake I see business owners make is managing their cash flow with their bank statements. I've seen business owners jump online to look at their current account balance, then go on a spending spree. Three days later, the bank is calling to talk about the negative cash balance in their account and the NSF checks that just came in.

Your bank balance is not your cash flow. Neither is your income statement, for that matter. Operating at a profit or loss is not the same as having a positive or negative cash flow. The most overlooked financial statement in small businesses is the statement of cash flows. My suggestion to every business owner is to become an expert in this one financial statement. The income statement and balance sheet are important to your accountant, and they provide you with a nice report card on how your business is doing. But ultimately, cash is king. If you aren't paying attention to where your cash is, what it's being used for, and where it is coming from, you will find out quickly the pain of having no cash!

Your statement of cash flows will break down how your cash is used in your business. It takes into account things like investments, financing, and how well you manage your operating cash. If you are like most business owners, you get very frustrated when your accountant can't give you a straight answer about why your business is running short on money. Reconciling the difference between "net income" and your bank account balance can end up including a string of accounting terms that all sound like number tricks—accrual basis, depreciation, days outstanding, paid in capital, disbursements, etc. The statement of cash flows will help.

The first section of your statement of cash flows is the most important. It shows the cash flow your business creates through normal operations. It gets rid of all the accounting number games. It is all about your actual expenses, your actual sales, when you pay your bills, and when you receive money from your customers. It strips away all of the other nonsense and gives you an idea about whether or not the normal operations of your business are bringing in more money than they pay out. This section is a rock star for business owners who are trying to get a hold on their wasteful spending.

The rest of the statement will show you how much money you as the owner are putting in and taking out along with any major asset purchases and long-term financing you may be involved in. Unless you are very active on these fronts, these sections probably won't give you much insight on your cash.

There are a lot of tools and resources available to you if you are willing to take the time to use them. In your business, you most likely have vendors and service providers you rely on. These companies are helping to define your marketplace. Get to know them. Understand their business models and how they influence change. Software vendors are a great place to start. In order to provide you with the software you need, they spend a great amount of time, energy, and resources researching market trends. Take advantage of their knowledge. Visit their conferences and utilize any training they sponsor. Develop a relationship with an accountant you trust. Review all of your financial statements and ask questions.

But even having the best resources won't be enough if you aren't willing to change your spending behaviors. If you don't have enough cash in your business, then you need to make changes today—like drop this book and make a phone call. I guarantee you every business wastes money, even yours. It's up to you to find the waste and get rid of it.

17

Why do we have such bad luck?

You Don't Have Bad Luck; You Make Bad Decisions.

Would you believe that bottled water could bring down a business?

For a time, I worked for a small business in a small community. Both the business and the community thought they were bigger than they really were. The business owner had visions of being the biggest company in the region. It was an ambitious goal, to be sure, but it's better to aspire for greatness than to settle for mediocrity. He had carved out a nice little niche on the fringe of the industry, but it only appealed to a small number of people.

The community was like any other, and while it tried to be very metropolitan, its greatest strength was its small-town feel. It developed several events to try and put it on the map. While it continued to try to attract new businesses and events, it was a town of less than fifty thousand people and could only support so much growth.

In a way, the business and the community were mirror images of each other. They each had aspirations of being much bigger and appealing to a wider audience. But the strengths of each of them only appealed to a small market.

This business owner was very focused on his vision. Over and over, he would tell anyone who would listen about how big his company was going to be. He had discussions with community leaders about how his business would be a stepping-stone to other industries moving into the area. Those who really wanted to grow the community saw him as a champion of their movement, which allowed him to reach several leadership positions within the community. Being popular and being liked are, of course, two different things, but for this part of the story his popularity led to very consistent growth in his business. The business was becoming one of the big fish in this small pond.

The tactics he used to grow his business ruffled the feathers of some long-established business owners. While there was a strong group of business owners that wanted the community to grow, there were far more who wanted to see the community retain its small-town feel. Instead of a champion of growth, this business owner was seen as aggressive about achieving his goals, and his number-one goal was to be the next big thing.

This is where the water comes in to play. Our business owner had about twelve employees. Over the course of a few weeks, he noticed that his employees had started bringing in their own water bottles. Seeing an opportunity to build team and company morale, he decided to hire a water service to bring in bottled water once a week. At the suggestion of one of his salespeople, he chose a current client to provide the water. This was not one of those big moment decisions that required a detailed analysis. It was done, implemented, forgotten.

The whole process was very well received. It seems so simple, providing water to your employees, but even small gestures can have a major impact on the happiness of others.

Time went by, and the water consumption at the office went up. In fact, it more than doubled. Then suddenly, the water service stopped. There was no explanation or meetings about the water. Just as quickly as the decision was made to bring it in, the decision was made to cancel it.

Rumors started among the employees. Some people said that the costs went up and the owner decided not to pay it anymore. Others had heard that the water company started using a competitor so the business owner fired them out of spite. Either way, morale among the employees fell.

Word spread in the community about the water service being canceled as well. One of the consequences of a small community is that everyone knows everyone. When something like this happens, especially with a high-profile member of the community, people start talking. Rumors started in the community along the same path as the ones started by the employees. No one knows for sure what the real story is behind this decision, but the water company did switch to a competitor, and eventually everyone believed that was why they were fired. Instead of being the champion for growth, this business owner was now perceived as a spoiled child. The reputation of the company was now tarnished.

With revenue growth slowing, customer service falling, and a new focus on cost cutting, the owner struggled to find answers. Refusing to believe that one decision as small and insignificant as water could have any effect on his business, he continued to press and look for quick fixes. With the benefit of hindsight, we now know this small decision led to a series of problems. Revenue slowed because the community no longer trusted this company's sales team. Service fell because the employee morale sank.

In the end, the company survived and the damage was repaired. The goals were lowered, and the focus shifted to keeping the doors open rather than being the biggest company in the region. In the grand scheme of things, water didn't destroy a business, but it illustrates a glaring issue most business owners overlook: cause and effect.

As an expert in momentum and how it affects businesses, I have made it a point to continually study cause and effect. Newton's law says that for each action there is an equal and opposite reaction. Well that's not entirely true. In business, I would argue that for every action there is a multitude of effects that need to be accounted for.

How we make our decisions is an important part of momentum. What drives your decision making? In the heat of the moment, you don't have the time to analyze every possible scenario or rationalize your decisions. Are you going to follow your instincts? What if your instincts tell you to hit the brakes? Too often businesses lose momentum because they hit the brakes when they should be accelerating through the problem. To improve your decision making, we need to improve your instincts.

What if today you were face to face with a difficult decision? Not so long ago, most people used honor as a way to define their actions. Deals were struck with a handshake and the integrity of their reputation. Today we require twenty-page legal agreements signed by both parties before we'll do anything. In our childhood stories of honor, we see how the hero sacrifices his or her own personal success in order to the right thing. We elevate that sacrifice as the model for how we should all act. But when we are in the moment, how often are we looking for the "right" decision or the "right for me" decision?

For most people decision making is based on our past experiences and our expectations of the future. Trust has been replaced with cynicism. Either we've been fooled in the past and don't want to repeat that, or we are afraid of being fooled for the first time. An unfortunate side effect of our cynicism is that we close ourselves off to others. When you can't openly trust other people, how will you develop meaningful relationships with them?

Over time, this withdrawal affects our other decision-making processes. We become much more selfish about our needs and wants. Instead of thinking of the greater good or the effect our decisions will have on others, we focus on what we want right now. In those stories of honor, decisions and actions were considered by how they would affect the reputation of an entire family. Sons didn't want to dishonor their fathers by showing cowardice or selfishness and so on. The decision-making process was more about what was "right" or "good" and less about what you wanted right now.

Think of the last time you gave a person a raise. For Newton to be right, the only reaction to that act would be the opposite effect of giving money to the employee—which is reducing the money the company has in the bank. Newton and accounting must have gotten along wonderfully. But that's not how it works with people. That employee can view the raise in many ways—happy for the extra money, offended that it was less than expected, angry that it took so long to be rewarded, and on and on. Now, look at how those reactions can affect the rest of your business. The offended person will complain loudly to his or her coworkers and create morale problems. The angry person may try to sabotage the company by providing bad service or by possibly stealing. The happy person may reward the company with loyalty and extra effort. Then think about how your other employees react to how this employee is behaving. The repercussions will continue to build and expand throughout your entire organization until the next event starts a new chain reaction.

The first lesson in cause and effect is one of the hardest to learn. We are all a result of our own actions. If you eat a bunch of junk food and don't exercise, you are going to gain weight. If you choose to spend your time and money inside of casinos gambling, eventually you are going to find yourself broke (because like it or not, the house always wins). If you dedicate yourself to learning and reading books, you are going to be smarter.

Our actions are based on the decisions we make and the values we hold. Values hold a very high place in the decision-making process. We base most of our decisions on our perception of right or wrong and the importance we place on doing the "right" thing. That perception is provided to us through the values we have developed throughout our life. Given the choice, someone who values family strongly will choose to spend a quiet evening at home rather than going out for drinks with coworkers. That choice, based on that person's values, determined the action. The action creates who we are as people or even as a business. Still following?

Now we'll take this a step further. You are where you are in life because of the choices you have made. Let that sink in, and really think about it. Are you as successful as you had hoped you would be? Is your business where you want it to be? Your success is based solely on the decisions you have made. It has nothing to do with the decisions or actions made by others. You are responsible for you.

Why do so many successful people talk about having goals as a key ingredient for their success? Because having that one key thought, or that one key value, guides and controls their decisions and actions. They reached their success by focusing all of their energy on taking the right actions. When obstacles pop up, they act and find solutions. They look at what actions or decisions they made that led to the obstacle and learn from them. Successful people understand clearly that they are in control of their life.

What about the people who seem to always live life with their head in the clouds? These are the dreamers of the world; they have wonderful plans but never fully invest themselves in getting started. Unfortunately, they aren't focused on taking actions. They see the world differently. When something happens to them, it is always someone else's fault. Accountability flies right out the window. Obstacles pop up and these people wilt. Are they afraid to take the action needed? Eventually they turn into victims and look for an excuse to quit. They are looking for someone to hand them their dream.

Looking for fault and blame when things go wrong is a waste of time. Success and achievement rest entirely with you and the decisions you make. In my workshops this would be the point where I ask the group to list ten decisions they have made (good or bad) that have directly led them to where they are today. I would suggest you do the same thing. Until you can relate your decisions and actions to your position in life, you'll never have the accountability needed to achieve something great.

If you are holding out for some exception to this rule, you won't find it with me. I hear overweight people who say it's a gland problem or that it is hereditary. I hear unemployed people who say they are too qualified to get a job. I hear people with jobs complain that they can never get a promotion because they have a bad boss. What I really hear are excuses.

It is an epidemic in our society that we try to make everyone feel special. In youth sports there are no winners and losers anymore. Participation is all that counts. Every player on a team is guaranteed playing time, whether he or she earned it or not. Hard work, making the right choices, and committing to an action used to be rewarded with success. Now, you get to show up and get the exact same benefit as everyone else. Why in the world would people want to work hard or do anything of significance if they don't get recognized for the achievement? It's time for everyone to jump up and realize they are the results of their own thinking.

I used to be quite a bit overweight. It's hard to commit yourself to losing weight and getting in shape. I've been there. Sometimes it's easier to not try. If you believe you have a glandular problem, you have a built-in excuse for never losing weight. Trying means you might fail. So, you allow your thoughts to keep you overweight because you don't want to put out the effort to change. It's no different with your business. If you believe it's all someone else's fault, you will never be able to take the right actions to fix the problem.

This is the power of understanding how your decisions affect your life and your success. You don't want it to be someone else's fault. As much as it may hurt your ego to think you made a bad decision, at least you can learn from it. I had a business owner tell me that he was in bad shape because he had an employee who stole thousands of dollars from him. He was willing to blame that employee for the problems he was having. Guess what, Buddy, you hired him, and you failed to check his work or put in place any controls to keep him from stealing. It's your fault, not his; now learn from it and fix it. Take action.

I stumbled across a quote that says, "To fight a bull when you are not scared is nothing. And to not fight a bull when you are scared is nothing. But to fight a bull when you are scared is something." Don't let your fear of failure or your overconfidence keep you from doing the right things for yourself and your business.

Cause and effect is the principle building block of better decision making. Your decisions have the biggest impact on the momentum of your company. Like any business owner, you are making hundreds of decisions each day. Since each decision has a cascading tree of effects, you need to make sure you're decision making skills are top-notch.

I hope you took the time to write down some of the decisions you have made recently. In order to understand cause and effect in a business sense, I want you to work with several of these decisions. I created a chart based on the water incident from the beginning of the chapter:

Decision: Cancel Water Delivery Service

Internal

Who Is Affected?	Direct or Indirect	Effect on Momentum	Effect on Goals
P & L	D	+	+
Employees	D	-	-

External

Who Is Affected?	Direct or Indirect	Effect on Momentum	Effect on Goals
Client	D	-	-
Customers	I	-	-
Community	I	-	-

In this case, I have done a quick analysis of the potential effects of this decision. I broke the tables into two different categories—internal and external. Internal effects are those that are seen inside of the company. It could be all employees or just a section of your employees. It could be the building your business is in, the technology you use, or an accounting effect. In this instance, I'm assuming that by canceling the water service I will cut expenses, which will have a positive effect on my profit and loss statement.

The external effects are on all the entities or stakeholders that are outside of the company. So your clients, your vendors, and your suppliers are all examples of external stakeholders. How will this decision affect these people? In this chart, I marked them as having a negative effect on our business. Some of the worst decisions are made because the external effects are ignored. Don't skip this step.

I've seen decision trees that are much more elaborate and complex than this. Do what works for you. But the important part of this exercise is to look at the different layers of your business that each decision affects. If you only focus on the immediate gratification of the decision, in this case cutting costs, you miss out on how the decision may affect your employees or your customers.

Looking at this table, it is easy to see how many negative effects this decision brings. In this context, it wouldn't seem right to go ahead and cancel the water service. But there might be other circumstances that aren't being represented here.

Chart each potential decision. In this case, you have the option of canceling the service or keeping the service. How will each decision affect the internal and external stakeholders of your company? What are the other factors that need to be addressed? Most importantly, are there alternative solutions?

I'm sure you don't have time to chart every decision you have to make. And it isn't even close to practical to do so. But do chart out several of your past decisions for practice. Chart out some of your major upcoming decisions. With some time, you'll be able to identify the first-level effects without charting.

Second- and third-level effects are more difficult to master. The chart we looked at dealt mostly with first-level effects. Second and third levels are generally your indirect effects. In our chart the customer being negatively impacted was a third-level effect. It was based on the fact that the employees weren't as happy at work. Because of this, the service level went down—the second-level effect. When service goes down, the customer experience is affected, and customer belief in your company is reduced. While this may seem like a logical progression, some third-level effects can be quite surprising.

Making decisions is all about choosing outcomes. Bad decision makers use the phrase "unexpected consequences" a lot. As in, "The decision seemed right at the time, but we encountered unexpected consequences." Spend any time at all watching financial networks, and you will find a CEO of a major company who is trying to explain why earnings are down. Eventually he or she will say there was no way to predict what will happen. Whether it is a down economy or new legislation or just a bad product idea, these are people who are looking for excuses to explain away a bad decision.

Thinking about all of these effects is the first step toward improving your decision making skills. But how well do you know your employees? What motivates them? What are their goals? What keeps them up at night? Don't guess. Don't generalize. Don't think you know what they are feeling just because you felt that way when you were in their place. Everyone is different, and everyone has had different experiences that shaped their values and decision making. Learn as much as you can about your employees—especially your key employees and the ones you trust with decision making.

What about the other stakeholders in your company? What do you know about your customers? Don't rely on a marketing profile. Get to know them personally. Maybe not all of them, but at least a few. Think about the needs and goals of your suppliers. Your community and your industry need your attention. If you want to be great at decision making, you need to have a wider understanding of your company.

Before we go too much further, I want you to grab a piece of paper and a marker and write down these words: *Remember the Water Cooler!* Hang this paper up in your office. Tape it to your bathroom mirror. Make it part of your screensaver. All of us get to a point where we truly believe we are making the right decisions and we know how everyone will react. Don't let yourself believe it. Stay vigilant. Your decisions are building your momentum. It can be negative momentum or it can be positive momentum, but never doubt it is building with every decision. The water cooler was a silly little decision that shouldn't have made much of a difference. But it did. It reached out from the break room and upset a community. It affected customer service. It stalled sales. It changed the course of a company. It wasn't bad luck, no matter how much they wanted to believe it was.

It was a bad decision, based on a person acting out without thinking of the consequences. It was the type of mistake you won't make in the future.

18

How do I get my employees to stop making mistakes?

Close Your Doors And Fire All Your Employees.

There are two types of mistakes: mistakes of effort and mistakes of laziness or incompetence. Lazy mistakes need to be fixed immediately. Employees who consistently make dumb mistakes over and over because they are lazy or refuse to learn from them need to find another place of employment. But those aren't the mistakes that can affect the direction of a business. Put in place a good quality-assurance plan, and you can identify and eliminate those procedural mistakes.

No, the mistakes that make the biggest impact on a business are the mistakes of effort. These mistakes are the ones that people make when they are actually trying to do something that matters. I've seen people lose their jobs because they offered too big of a discount to a customer who was upset and making a scene. Maybe it's against company policy, but at least that employee was trying to resolve the problem. Business owners that focus on and punish those types of mistakes are on the short path to a losing business model.

While I was writing this book, one of my friends asked me how the process was going. I told him it was easy; I just had to pick the exact perfect word seventy thousand times and then I'd be done. Funny joke. The fact is, this book and thousands others would never get published if that was the goal of every writer. It's about getting the best out of you and then moving forward.

You can sit back and wait for perfect conditions. You can deliberate until you are absolutely sure you have not just the right answer, but the perfect answer. You can hold your team or your employees to the standard of perfection. But time won't wait for you. Your customers won't wait for you. Your competition won't wait for you. You will sit on the sideline waiting for perfection while everyone else finds success through action. Life and business will not wait for you. If you want to survive, you will have to act knowing that you could make a mistake.

Winter in the Pacific Northwest can be very unpredictable. From freezing rain to blizzards to arctic cold, we never know year to year what to expect. This particular year was a fairly mild winter, not too much snow and not a lot of cold weather. My parents are about a two-hour car ride away, so in bad winters the holidays are spent with phone calls and pictures. But this year, my wife and I decided to make the journey. We bundled up our young son and set off to spend the holidays with Grandma and Grandpa.

Twenty minutes into the drive, we began the climb up the first of two mountain passes. Halfway up the hill, I rounded a corner and had a split second of panic before my instincts took over. A semi was jackknifed on the freeway and sliding toward us. There were two other cars that were spun around and facing the wrong way. There was debris in the road, and I could see the shine of solid ice covering most of the roadway. All of this was happening in slow motion, and I started to feel our tires slipping.

Anyone's initial reaction is going to be to avoid danger—hit the brakes, swerve, get out of the way. But it is those instincts that can lead to a worse situation. Hitting the brakes meant I would lose forward momentum and start sliding. Swerving meant I would lose control of the car and wouldn't know where my momentum would take me. Getting out of the way was almost impossible unless I did the one thing that was completely against anyone's instincts. I sped up.

By accelerating I kept my momentum going forward, and I kept control of the car. I was able to make a small correction and avoid the semi. I straddled the debris on the road and watched one of the cars literally slide just to the right of our front fender as I made it through the corner.

This story is always a reminder for me about how our instincts and our reflexes can sometimes work against us. If I had given in to my natural reaction, our car would have been wrecked just like those others. Who knows if we would have been hurt or not. It is a lesson that needs to be remembered by business owners as well.

I could have hesitated. I could have given in to the survival instinct and slowed down trying to avoid the mistakes coming at me. But I chose action. I chose to do something against the grain with the hopes of avoiding the worst part of the disaster. I took a chance not everyone would be willing to take, and it paid off for us. But if I had been worried about making mistakes, could I have made that choice? I don't know.

It's hard enough to get things done in the workplace without the added pressure of perfection. There are two sayings that have stuck with me for years: "Mistakes are proof you are trying" and "Sign the damn painting." The first saying is a reminder to me that you have to focus on taking action every day. Sitting on the sideline is never an option, so go out there, do something, and if you make a mistake then that's a good thing. It proves you are taking action and trying to get something done. The second saying is a reminder that you eventually have to finish a project. You can mess around forever with something hoping to get it just right, but at some point you have to accept it as good enough and move on to the next project. In other words, sign the painting and get another canvas.

Instead of focusing on mistakes, you need to recognize action in the workplace and hold it up as the example. Get your workforce used to the idea that action is more important than anything else. Set the example by digging in and getting active in your own business. Accept failure as a signpost of everyone trying something new. As I heard over and over growing up, if you aren't failing, then you aren't pushing yourself far enough.

Make sure employees know that you expect them to anticipate the needs of the company or the client and to take action. Whether that action is to alert the appropriate department or to create a new product, your employees need to act. Some of the best ideas for business will come from your front lines. They deal with your customers all day, every day. Encourage them to speak up and take actions that might never be discussed in a board room.

Second, you need to encourage ideas. I can remember hearing a business owner addressing his staff and saying that he was looking for new creative ideas for the business. When I talked to the employees to see what ideas they had come up with, most of them passed. Apparently in previous staff meetings, the same business owner ripped apart each idea that was presented right then and there. No one was willing to come up with new ideas after that.

To encourage ideas, you have to allow people to explore them far enough to see if they are feasible or not. As hard as it may be, you will have to create an environment that believes in the ideas of others enough that it is OK for them to fail. From the failure, new ideas will be born. Celebrate the success of ideas that add value to the company. If an idea creates a new asset, then monetary rewards, promotions, or just plain public recognition is in order. If an idea fails, encourage the employee to take those lessons and push forward to a new idea. Punishing a failure is a surefire way to stifle the creative process in your organization.

Fear of failure is the biggest obstacle to overcome in this process. As the owner, you have the option of picking an idea and failing big and failing fast without hurting the overall company. At that point you can head up the first "failure investigation" and set the example for future reviews. Showing how failure will be handled can alleviate a lot of the stress that goes along with being creative. You don't want your people behaving out of fear if you want truly unique ideas.

To help add speed to your company culture, make sure you emphasize results. Some managers are very content with the idea of busywork. Too often, "as long as people are busy, they are productive" is the management mantra. Not only is that complete garbage, but it is destructive to your company. Work that doesn't produce tangible results is wasting the time and resources of your company. You don't need that type of thinking in your business. Make sure everyone understands that results are what matters, and then reward them appropriately when they produce.

Taking action when the outcome is unknown is what separates market leaders from market followers. If you knew you were going to be successful 99 percent of the time, wouldn't you go forward? What about 80 percent or 60 percent? When you find the level you are comfortable with, you've discovered what is called your risk tolerance. Only you know what you can live with in terms of risk. But if you are waiting for sure things, your business will never make any major movements in the market.

So the real question is this: Can you commit to an action without knowing the outcome?

I'm not talking about taking foolish risks or making random decisions. But waiting until you know for sure what the market is going to do is just a recipe for mediocrity. You don't have to be first to market with a product; you can follow others. You don't have to anticipate what your customers are going to need; you can wait for them to tell you. You don't need create anything new; you can just repackage what other people do. You can also have a second-rate company that struggles to make ends meet every year. The problem you will consistently face in our on-demand society is that most customers won't wait for you to catch up. They will buy from your competitors, and you'll be closing your doors.

To be the best in your industry and build consistent momentum, you must know your business, and you must know your customers. Have confidence in your knowledge and use it to create new opportunities. Sure, you might fail. But you also might change the marketplace and dominate it. Trust your employees to make the right decisions. Trust them to learn from their mistakes. Trust in the fact that many really cool innovations were discovered by mistake. Remember, mistakes are proof that you are trying.

Letting your employees act without certainty isn't always a gamble. I'm not telling you to turn everyone loose and wait to see what happens. But you can lighten up the pressure a bit. You have to avoid that phenomenon where the company analyzes every decision to death. You can't have the expectation that you'll know everything before it's time to act. You have to be ready to make a decision and move your company forward when there is still some doubt. And you have to allow some freedom for your employees to act on their own if you ever want to benefit from their creativity.

I have never met the person who knows everything. We all rely on our instincts at times to guide us when we aren't sure what we are supposed to be doing. Trusting your intuition or instincts is easier for some people. Business owners are natural risk takers, but employees don't always feel comfortable going out on a limb based solely on their own intuition. Develop a mentorship program in the office to help employees work on high-risk, high-reward projects. Because the "mentor" ends up with the full responsibility for the success or failure of the project, employees are more likely to participate without fear. Train the employees on how to manage these types of high impact projects. Over time, you will see new leaders come forward, and your culture will be focused on results, performance, and growth.

Completing a project or task is one of the hardest things for anyone to do. We can get things started, we can work hard on them, and we can work hard on them, and we can work hard on them. But when the deadline comes and it's time to turn it in, there is always one more revision, one more addition, one more feature that needs to go into it. Your employees are just more comfortable working hard on it. Turning it in means their effort and results are going to be graded. More than any other factor in business, this is the main reason projects go over budget and miss deadlines. No one wants to sign off on the completed project.

If you think I'm going to say it's OK for projects to be "good enough," then you will be disappointed. Every task or project or assignment has a purpose. That purpose must be met, without exception. Projects that are overdue and over budget that still don't meet the stated goals need to be addressed immediately. That behavior needs to be corrected, no matter whose feelings might get hurt. But a project that is completed and meets the stated goals is a success.

But this is where some decision makers make their biggest mistake. The project is a success, but it wasn't done the way that decision maker would have done it. So the project gets picked apart, the differences in how it was implemented are held up as mistakes, and the project is sent back for revisions. Now it's over budget, overdue, and the project team is under pressure. More mistakes are made as they try to work in the "suggestions" from the decision maker, and the project ends up falling apart.

How well do you think future projects are going to go? Confidence is low, and no one wants to take on a high-profile role in a project because no one wants to get treated like a failure. As the business owner, you need to make sure your focus is on meeting stated goals, not on the process of how the stated goals are met. It's a big leap of faith, but if you spend all your time worrying about the minutiae of how things get done, how will you ever find the time to set the proper course for your business?

A funny thing happens when you focus all your attention on mistakes—you find them. Then because you are so focused on the mistake, you actually help create more mistakes. But if you focus on results, amazingly you will get results. And even better, the mistakes you were worried about to begin with start disappearing all on their own.

19

Why can't anyone make a marketing brochure that works?

Because You Have No Idea How To Market Your Business.

Let me guess, you spent a couple hundred bucks getting a brochure designed. Then you spent another couple hundred getting them printed up and delivered. You pulled them out of the box and showed them around to your employees, family, and friends. Everyone oooh'd and ahhh'd over them and told you how fancy and professional they looked. You grabbed a stack of the brochures and walked out the door to show the world how great your company is. You even started to wonder if you could handle all the new business these brochures were going to bring you. Dumbass.

After a few weeks of dropping off brochures at different places, you started to realize that maybe these brochures aren't going to bring a tidal wave of new customers. The real pain happens when you sit back and start thinking about how many of your brochures ended up in a trash can. Your money, literally thrown away. About half of you learned your lesson at this point and decided brochures are a waste of money, and you tried something else. The other half of you blamed the designer of the brochure and hired someone else to make a new one—one that worked. You paid even more for this second set and still got the same results. And again, it was the designer's fault. Dumbass.

Earlier I told you that advertising is a tool of marketing, and it is a very expensive tool. Brochures, flyers, Web sites, business cards, and mailers are all tools of marketing, too. And they can be just as expensive. If you just do one-off runs of a brochure, it's going to fail. Just like advertising, you can't run one ad in one newspaper and expect your phone to ring off the hook for the next month. Marketing doesn't happen in a vacuum. Just as you are trying to get your message out, your competitors are doing the exact same thing. In fact, even companies that aren't your direct competitors are competing with you for the attention of your customers. With all the marketing messages out there, it's no wonder that customers are training themselves to tune it all out.

So if you are like most of the people I work with, this is where you ask the obvious question. If consumers don't believe in ads and are training themselves to be skeptical of marketing messages, how do you ever develop a marketing plan? Well you're in luck, I'm going to give you a crash course on the most powerful tool in the marketing toolbox—the campaign.

In order to get a person to buy, you have to satisfy three requirements. The first requirement is that you target the right customer. Secondly you have to create an offer that appeals to the senses that drive buying behavior, and finally you have to create urgency behind the offer. A campaign is the perfect vehicle to satisfy all three components.

When you put the focus on generating revenue with your marketing plan, you don't give yourself much room for wasteful spending. You absolutely have to identify your target customer. Not just the standard demographics either. Understand where your customer gets his or her news. Where does he shop? What types of Web sites does she view on a daily basis? When the campaign starts, you have to be able to get your message directly to your target customers. You aren't casting a wide net here. You want to reach those people who are most likely to buy from you right now.

Believe me, the time, energy, and yes, money you invest at this stage will be worth it in the end. This type of research doesn't have to be overly complicated either. Get out and talk to people. Tell them what you do and why it's important. Call on your existing customers and get feedback from them about why they buy from you. Absorb as much information as you can. When you understand whom you serve and why they want to buy, you will be ready to craft your message. And don't guess, and don't assume you already know your customers—that is lazy, passive marketing.

When making a buying decision, people are more likely to buy if they have an emotional response to the product or service. Consumers buy with emotion and justify with logic. So if you are able to create a compelling offer that touches on the emotions of your target audience, you will sell considerably more than trying to appeal to the logic of your customer.

You don't have very long to make an impression on your potential customers. If your message doesn't grab their attention and create some form of response, these prospects will move on without giving you, your company, or your products a second thought. So don't waste any time talking about you or your company.

In fact, you probably want to skip talking about your products and services, too. They have very little to do with why your customers buy from you. Are you surprised by that? If so, you need to go back to step one and talk to more of your customers. People buy the transformation your product or service provides; they could care less about the product.

If I was creating an ad about a wristwatch, I could talk about its features. I could tell you that it has Swiss precision, a durable finish, water resistance to three hundred meters, and a twenty-year warranty. Are you ready to buy? What if I told you about how this watch is the status symbol of this decade and has been worn on the runways of New York and Paris?

The second message only speaks to a few people who are interested in high fashion. Personally, I could care less about a watch as a status symbol. But if I did, I'd be more likely to buy from the second message than the first. In fact, I'd probably end up spending quite a bit more money just to have that watch. The features would be how I logically justified the purchase after the fact.

It works with any product. Don't focus on the features of your product in your message. Focus on the transformation it creates. Reach people on an emotional level, and they will respond. Do people buy fitness equipment because they like to work out? No. They buy it to lose weight and get in shape. That is the transformation.

In order to reach your target market on an emotional level, you have to understand the two motivators that create action in people. The first motivator is the removal of pain. We learn this at a very early age. If I touch a hot stove, I'm going to pull my hand back. I'm motivated to remove the pain. The second motivator is the pursuit of pleasure. We learn this over the course of a lifetime. Our pursuit of pleasure changes as our tastes and preferences change, but we will still buy and act in order to bring happiness into our lives.

Now the key here is that the removal of pain is ten times more powerful of a motivator than the pursuit of pleasure. So when you are crafting your marketing message, focus on the transformation your product or service provides and how it removes pain from your customer. Our watch removes the pain of not being accepted in the higher circles of fashion. Your product removes a pain in your customers' lives as well.

There is a simple formula to help you get started crafting this very powerful message. Even if you think your business provides a pursuit of pleasure style of product or service, you will get more sales and more leads if you rephrase your message as a way to solve a problem. To get started, fill in the blanks on this sentence: "**I help** (*target market*) **solve** (*identifiable problem*) **so that** (*perceived benefit*)."

We've already talked about the target market, so let's focus on the other two sections. What problem do you solve? This problem needs to be easily recognizable and accepted by your target market. Don't try and create a new problem that doesn't really exist. If you are marketing sunscreen to life guards, you can talk about the risk of sunburns and their link to skin cancer. But you couldn't market sunscreen to office workers because of radiation from fluorescent bulbs. Even if there is radiation, you are stepping into a debate in the workers' minds. Your message is completely lost.

Once you have identified the problem, then you need to show how your product solves it and why that is a benefit. This is the transformation your target market will feel once they have your product. "Our sunscreen protects against sunburns and skin cancer so that your face will retain its youth and clear complexion for years to come." See how you can easily get an emotional response from this type of message? It is infinitely more effective than talking about the technical aspects of how it blocks UV radiation and has a high SPF number.

Later in the campaign, you will want to build trust and authority in your products and services. This is where you would include things like testimonials or the quality and stability of your company. These types of messages build on the logic side of the decision-making process and are there to help your customers justify their emotional response to your message. You want to provide these reassurances, but not in the initial marketing message.

The final component of your campaign is to create urgency. A campaign runs for a specific period of time. You can run campaigns back to back, but each campaign has a definite start and finish date. There are several reasons for this, which we will discuss in a bit. But in order to build momentum with your campaign, you need to create an environment where your interested customers buy now.

Urgency starts with an irresistible offer. Remember, consumers are skeptical and cynical. If you don't reach them on an emotional level, they are going to ignore your message. But once they are hooked emotionally, your offer has to pass the logic test. You have to overcome any objections they may have.

An irresistible offer creates urgency by taking away any barriers your customers may use to avoid making a buying decision. It can be as simple as offering a guarantee on your work or a free trial. When you have a good idea about the challenges your target market faces daily, creating this offer becomes much easier.

One of the most common ways to create urgency is through special sales events or ongoing discounts. While they are somewhat effective, there is a sort of laziness about this type of deadline. "Buy now before we raise our prices" is never a good message to hot prospects. These people are ready to buy; they just need a little push. Don't cut your profit margin because you want to be lazy at the end of your campaign.

Creating exclusivity is a much better method of creating urgency. "By buying in the next two days, you are automatically enrolled in our private membership program that offers various features and benefits" is a much more creative form of urgency. Limited availability of the product or service is another way to create urgency. "We only have room for twenty people in our new training program, so be the first to order so that you are guaranteed a spot." None of these methods cut down on your profitability, but they do create a little added pressure on the customer to act now.

When you make the decision to run a marketing campaign, you are committing to a very structured process. I worked with one company that decided to do a campaign and quit after one mailing. If you are used to the old-school passive marketing strategies, a campaign mindset is going to be challenging for you.

Remember, every campaign has a beginning, middle, and end. You have to be willing to see it through to the end. The more planning you do, the better results you will see. Your campaign will never be successful if it continually stops, changes, and starts again.

A campaign is all about building momentum throughout the process. First you get your emotional marketing message out to your target market. Then you give them the reasons for working with you and present your irresistible offer. Finally, you create urgency with a limited-time window for added benefits and the campaign ends. At each stage, you are building interest and anticipation. This leads directly to sales.

The main reason for having a definitive ending period in your campaign is to add to the urgency of your offer. It may be a false or arbitrary deadline, but in the customers' mind it creates an incentive to act now. But having an ending to the campaign offers many other benefits, too.

At the end of your campaign, you can review your results. It gives you a chance to look back at what worked and what didn't. Did you time your messages correctly? Was the target audience interested in the offer? This period of time needs to be used to correct any issues before you run the campaign again.

This is also a cooling-off period for your sales and operational staff. When you bring on several customers at a time, it puts a lot of pressure on your team. Do you have the right number of support people to handle all the new requests? Is your inventory sufficient to handle the new sales? Use this time to work out the plan for handling your next campaign.

When you have everything ready internally, it's time to run your campaign again. As you improve each phase of your campaign, you will see consistent improvement in not only the volume but also the quality of the leads coming in. You will close more deals, you will attract more attention, and you will build more brand awareness as you continue to run your campaigns.

You have a lot of choices on how you are going to get your message out. Most of the books on marketing really focus on this aspect of the process, so I'm not going to spend too much time on this. But there are a few points that I think are important to look at in terms of building marketing momentum.

Make sure every message you create has some form of an offer and a call to action. This is the minimum requirement for all of your marketing. If your message is missing one or both of these, then you can be sure you are wasting your marketing dollars.

But don't neglect many of the more traditional ways of getting your message out. The more personal you get with your message and delivery, the better response you will have. Remember to get out and meet people face to face. E-mail marketing is fast, inexpensive, and impersonal. Picking up the phone and calling prospects may take longer, but it can add a personal touch to your campaign. Again, go back to being an active marketer rather than waiting for someone to find you.

The other big shift in marketing is using technology to become an educational resource in your industry. I am a big proponent of this method if it is done right. Nothing builds your audience faster than being respected as a thought leader in your industry.

Audio and video equipment has been dropping in price rapidly. You can pick up high-definition recording equipment with lights and screens for less than a thousand bucks. You can get high-quality microphones for less than fifty bucks. There are free software programs you can use to edit video and audio feeds. The social-media sites are great places to stream your training programs for free. It has never been so cost-effective to put together training programs as a way of generating sales.

Unfortunately, many businesses don't understand how to do this correctly. Many businesses don't even realize their training programs should be designed to generate more sales. Even if they are focused on generating more revenue, they end up offering training that contains the wrong information. Another advantage is using training as a way to retain customers or to provide added value after the sale. It's time to look at this as an easy way to take those trainings and turn them into momentum-building sales events.

The key to a powerful training program is to really connect with the pain or problems that are affecting your target audience. Just like your marketing message, you need to connect on an emotional level quickly in any of your training programs. When an audience makes an emotional connection with you, two important things happen. First, you instantly gain credibility. Second, you hold their interest.

Training only works if your audience is willing to believe in you as an authority on the topic. Ineffective speakers spend the first ten or fifteen minutes of a presentation talking about their credentials. They are trying to prove they belong as a thought leader in the industry. In those few minutes, they lose most of the buying public and hold on to others in the industry. In other words, they turn off their prospects and start training their competition.

Your resume has nothing to do with how you will be perceived in the training. Consumers are looking for answers and transformation. So instead of quoting your resume, talk about the symptoms everyone in your target market suffers from. An accountant might start her talk by telling the story of a client who was audited by the IRS and how the constant worry and concern around taxes affects everyone. Now she has connected on a typical fear and pain point for many, and she can continue talking about how that problem can be solved.

By introducing the symptoms of the problem the audience is experiencing, you have captured their attention. They are waiting for the solution from you, and now is the time you can start to explain why you are an expert in this field. Talk about successes you have had in the past. Bring up any testimonials you may have about you and your company. Just like your other marketing messages, you capture them with emotion and then help them justify choosing you with logic.

Bring the training back to the problem at hand by explaining the biggest myth in your industry. Or, if it's more appropriate, you can identify the biggest mistake people make when trying to overcome this problem. Again, you are building your credibility with the audience. By acknowledging that you understand the problem and have lived through the process of solving it, your audience begins to build a relationship with you. They will see you as one of them. You want them to be on the edge of their seats waiting for the answer to their very real, very serious problems.

Finally, you present the audience with the first step they need to take. Don't give them the whole process, but don't shortchange them either. No one likes going to a training and feeling like it was just an extra-long sales pitch. You need to give them a tried-and-true action step that will get them started on the path to the solution. But in the end, it is your product or service they need to finish the journey, so don't give away the whole process.

Before the training ends, make sure your audience knows how to contact you if they have questions or want to get more information about you and your products. If you are doing live, in-person trainings, make sure you are prepared to sell your products and services at the end of the training.

An online or recorded training program structured like this should be no more than twenty to thirty minutes including a brief Q and A period. This is the sweet spot for webinars and teleseminars. Any longer and you begin to lose the audience's attention. Shorter presentations feel much more like a sales pitch. Live trainings should be somewhere between thirty and forty-five minutes. In a live training, you can end up with many more questions, so the extra time can be used to give more people a chance to get answers.

Don't try to make it longer by throwing in "filler" content, or your training will lose impact and your audience won't connect strongly with you. Just provide the four keys I listed above and move on. This type of program is an amazing addition to any marketing campaign, so play around with the format and make it work for you and your business. Remember, all of your marketing strategies begin and end with a focus on generating more revenue. Be creative with how to get your message out, but be structured with the quality of the message.

It's time to let go of any hope that traditional marketing avenues are going to have a major impact on the success of small businesses going forward. The days when a clever headline and a provocative image could generate buzz and eventually a sale are done. If you want to reach your audience now, you have to go out and find them. Waiting around for them to find you is a sucker's game. You'll lose every time.

This is a consumer's market. Your customers can get products and services from anywhere at anytime. Where you can differentiate yourself is by proving that your company is worthy of their business. All of the shady companies and outright scams on the Internet have made consumers cautious about where they are willing to spend money. One message will never be enough to convince them you are a trustworthy company.

The power of the campaign is being able to get in front of potential customers several times. It gives you the chance to build credibility with your customers before asking them to make a purchasing decision. Creating a training program builds authority in the market. Together these powerful strategies will set you apart from all of your competition. This is the new face of marketing, and because these strategies are designed to be running continually, it is the easiest way to generate a pipeline of consistent leads.

And isn't that what your marketing is supposed to do?

20

Why can't I get support from local businesses?

Because You Haven't Proven Your Worth To Your Community.

I live in one of the most beautiful parts of the country. I know this not because I have traveled all over the country, but because everyone who comes to visit here claims it is the most beautiful countryside they have seen. I've never heard a visitor say, "Yeah, this is great, but if you want real beauty you should visit…" It just doesn't happen around here.

The blessing and curse of living in such a beautiful place is that everyone else wants to live here, too. We've seen amazing growth in our area, and with it we've seen the growth of small businesses. It can take you by surprise if you really drive around your town and look at all the small businesses that are hidden in plain sight. Every week I find at least a few new businesses that I had no idea existed.

The big box stores and the national retailers keep us from seeing all the other businesses that are making a go of it. Why is that? Part of it is marketing, but another part of it is the local influence these businesses have.

These big retailers and major national brands offer a lot of jobs. They offer a certain amount of security. As consumers we have a little more trust in the longevity of these big stores. If one of these stores ever had to close its doors, it would make national news. There would be analysis and commentary about the company. Experts would be on talk shows dissecting the effects this would have on the economy. It would take several months of sales to remove the inventory. The closing of a store would have an almost theatrical quality to it with an opening, a middle, the crescendo, and then the ultimate finality of the closed doors.

When a small business closes its doors, it happens very quietly. There may be a closing sale, but it will only get local press. These businesses close relatively quickly. You can be out of town for a mini vacation and completely miss the store getting closed. One day the business is there; the next day there is a for-lease sign in the window.

In 2009, when the recession was in full force, our community struggled like so many others. I can remember driving down some of our major streets with my son. We were counting the for-lease signs as we drove. What started as a harmless game turned into a serious discussion. It started when my son asked the simple question "Why are all of these businesses closed?"

As I told him, there are many reasons businesses fail. But it boils down to one thing—the business owner made the wrong choices. When the time came to make a big decision about the direction of the business, this owner failed. There are many business owners who don't understand the importance their business can play in the community. They look at the national brands in their community and decide they can't compete. And they believe they can't have an impact in the community because of the influence from these major corporations.

It's too bad really, because having a focus on creating an impact in the community is an amazing way to generate momentum and growth for small businesses. Too many business owners look at their business as an entity that exists to serve them. I've worked with several people who have this point of view about their business. But these are not bad or selfish people. They have a genuine concern for the success of their business and the people who work for them. It is some of the smaller, subtler actions that really create a distinction with these people. And I will say business owners who believe their business exists to serve themselves generally do not stay in business over long periods of time.

Business owners who have longevity understand their business exists to serve the community. I can hear objections now. "My business exists to serve my customers." Of course it does. That's why you are giving your services away for free and your employees are volunteering their time to you, right? No, you are in business to make money. Businesses provide services and products to solve the problems your customers have. But a business doesn't exist to only do that. The business must serve the community if it is going to have any longevity.

As a business owner, have you ever decided against working with a vendor because you weren't sure if they were going to be around in another year? It's a reasonable thought to have when you are evaluating vendors. You can't just focus on who offers the newest product or the best price. If that vendor isn't going to be around to support you, then you probably should find someone else. So if you aren't getting the local support you think you deserve, then maybe you should take another look at your business. Are you the type of business you would buy from?

I worked with a local gym that was just getting started. If you watch infomercials on TV for any period of time, you are going to realize there are only three types that exist—get rich quick, household gadgets, and diet and fitness. The diet and fitness category probably takes up as much time as all the others combined.

So how does a gym that is just getting started stand out from the crowd? Is there really a difference between any of these gyms? To them, absolutely. They all have a different method or a unique experience they offer. But to a consumer, it's all about results. The consumer is paying to get fit or to build muscle or lose weight. If one gym doesn't work, there are hundreds of other options available. So this gym went a different route. They decided to become very active in the community.

Within a couple of weeks of opening the doors, the owners had joined several community groups. Alone this isn't unique or special, but they were active participants in these groups. One of the groups was focused on revitalizing their area of town. Taking the lead, this gym started hosting outdoor parties in their parking lot.

Anyone driving by could stop and join in with the festivities for free. They had outdoor fitness classes with a stage in the parking lot. Imagine driving by and seeing twenty people dancing and exercising on and around a stage. Even if they didn't get people to stop, they got their attention. People started thinking about that gym as something more than just a place to exercise.

During these parties, they closed the side road next to the gym and put up a portable basketball hoop. While the music was playing and the dancers were going, you had pickup basketball games. The trainers at the gym were inside giving demonstrations and talking about the techniques they used. Nutritionists and masseuses were also on site to offer free advice and demonstrations. With their passion for animals, the owners partnered up with the local humane society and put on adopt-a-thon sessions during these block parties.

While this seems like a great "grand opening" stunt, I'm here to say this had nothing to do with their grand opening. They offered some type of event like this once a month for an entire summer. Eventually other businesses joined in, and it became a bigger event. Every time it paid for itself with new memberships. But the most important thing it did was to cement the gym's reputation as a strong member of the community that planned to be there serving its customers for a long time.

Think about the things you have an interest in. Are there ways to get your company involved in some of these community events? Think about charities and causes you believe strongly in, and find ways to support them. While sponsoring events and putting your logo on a banner may be the easiest thing, you should try to find other ways to actively participate in the cause.

Are there ways you can educate the community on your industry? This gym worked hard to get articles published in the local papers talking about the importance of nutrition and fitness. These were not articles designed to be advertisements. The articles were authentic attempts to help readers understand the importance of a healthy lifestyle. The end result is potential customers recognizing the gym as a destination for expert advice.

As the gym gained popularity in the community, their membership grew. Because of their involvement in the community, their reputation continued to expand as a solid corporate citizen. They were looked to for leadership in many areas of the community. In their second year, several other fitness centers closed down. Because of the reputation of this gym, they were able to gain many of those customers who were left without a gym. The momentum of their image in the community has allowed them to not just survive but also to outlive their competitors.

When the phrase "corporate citizenship" comes up, many business owners cringe. I see it in their eyes before they even say it. For some reason, the term is attached to charity, recycling, the green initiative, and other similar terms. In short, for many business owners corporate citizenship is seen as a major expense, a major hassle, and something no one has time for. But still, these same business owners wonder why they always struggle month to month finding quality leads and converting more sales.

Those who understand the power of corporate citizenship see it in a different light. When the term comes up, their eyes twinkle and the corners of their mouths turn up. Excitement builds because these business owners see it as a source of abundance. It fills the company with a strong higher purpose, it inspires others in the community, and just as important, it brings in new customers willing to hand over their money.

We talked earlier about the presence of the big brands and the big retailers in a community. Each of these companies started small. They were able to build a huge following and support in the communities they served. It's no different than the path any other small business would need to follow. Businesses, large and small, have a responsibility to the community they reside in. If you aren't willing to accept that responsibility for your business, then maybe you aren't cut out to be a business owner.

Most small businesses start out as owner/operator companies. It's a one-man or a one-woman shop until the business grows enough to hire some help. Once you hire an employee, your business becomes about more than you. It has taken root in the community, and that community is relying on you as the business owner to act in a responsible manner.

That employee is now dependent on you for a job. With your growth, you are now buying services and products inside the community. Those businesses are dependent on you for income. You are selling services and products in the community, and they are counting on you to deliver. It is a lot of pressure to handle, but it is also very rewarding when you succeed.

Now think about all those businesses that had to close their doors. The owner failed the community—their employees, their vendors, their customers, and themselves. The decisions you make in your business affect more than just you and more than just your pocketbook. You need to account for all of those stakeholders inside and outside the company.

Maybe it's easier if we spend some time defining the community that each business serves. The community obviously includes the collection of people, businesses, customers, and vendors that exist in your area of influence. If you are a small business, that may just include the town you are in. For larger businesses, it may be a region or a nation. But it doesn't stop there. Your community also includes the employees in your organization.

Does this mean you can't fire an employee? No. In fact, it means you have to be willing to make the tough decisions about employees for the benefit of everyone else. I've been involved with a lot of decision makers who just couldn't make the decision to get rid of bad employees. It's easy when they break a rule or upset a customer and the choice is made for you. But what about those employees who just aren't good at their job? The ones who are well liked on a personal level, but no one wants to work with them because they don't produce? Are you willing to let them go for the benefit of the rest of the workforce?

Your employees are looking to you to be fair and reasonable. Allowing a bad employee to stay on because you are afraid to fire someone is not fair to the other employees who are working hard. Your responsibility to the company is to ensure its longevity. Most of your employees will be focused on the short-term, day-to-day decisions. You have to keep an eye on the long-term direction of the company. If you let a bad employee stay on, you could end up losing some of your good employees, and then your business ends up in trouble. When you are focused on long-term growth, anything that pulls you back has to go—whether it's a bad employee or just one who isn't quite good enough. Be willing to make that tough choice.

It is easy to look at the example of my community gym and see how they influenced their community and got involved with a local nonprofit. When you are actively participating in these circles, your reputation will grow inside your community. But there are some less charitable things you need to do in order to be a good corporate citizen.

It may seem selfish, but your business needs to make money—lots of it. A business that is barely able to pay the bills will struggle to commit fully to its community. You need to look at the financials of your business and make sure you are being responsible with how the money is being spent. You don't have to be an expert in finance or accounting, but you do need to have a basic understanding of how to handle the income and expenses of your business.

Many business owners, at the advice of their tax people, run a lot of personal expenses through the business. Have a car? Make it a company car and get a deduction. Taking a vacation? Meet with potential clients so you can get a deduction. There are a lot of strategies like that (please don't try these without talking to a CPA—I am not one, I don't pretend to be one, and I know enough about taxes to know that you shouldn't take advice from me in a book!), and while they may be good for your tax bill, they aren't always good for your business.

Business success is about abundance. It's about having enough to share with others, so in your business you need to create abundant resources. This means you need to focus on investing dollars in your business first. Too often, business owners are pulling money out of the business accounts to cover personal expenses. If you don't have enough money to cover your expenses, give yourself a raise. A raise can be budgeted and is consistent for the business. It is the "once in a while" expenses that kill the cash flow of many small businesses.

It may sound counterintuitive to talk about making money in the same context as being a good corporate citizen, but they really are the same thing. If your business runs out of money, you are going to have to close the doors. You can make a lot of really dumb decisions when you have a healthy cash flow and still survive. If your cash flow is bad, you have no room for error.

With a positive cash flow, you will be able to spend more time actively helping your community. You will be able to work with nonprofits and charities to help expose more people to the greatness of your business. Your employees will find the security they are looking for and will be able to perform at their highest levels. In a short period of time, you could find your business influencing your community.

It's when you start to have a voice and an influence in your community that you will start to really build momentum. You may still be a small business, but in your community you will be building the reputation that is normally reserved for the big retail companies. Instead of being perceived as a small business, you will be seen as a stable member of the community. And wasn't that the goal from the very beginning?

21

When will things settle down so I can finally grow my business?

Never. So Build Your Business Anyway.

t was 2009, and the recession was in full force. You couldn't escape the TV coverage of the market crashes and the constant debate about whose fault it was and how it could ever be fixed. As I was flipping through channels, I stopped on a news panel discussing the economy. Specifically, they were talking about why small business was struggling and how to get the economy moving again. Three people spoke, each with a different outlook on the problem.

The first person was a financial consultant, and he said the major problem was that banks were not lending any money. Credit had dried up, and the regulations were too tight on the banks. The second person represented a trade group and said the problem was that demand had fallen off a cliff. Consumers had simply stopped buying, leaving businesses unable to generate any new revenue. These two had valid points, but nothing out of the ordinary. In other words, I was ready to change the channel.

But before I could, the third person struck a chord with me. She was a business owner. Her complaint was that there was too much uncertainty in the market. No one knew what the government was going to do, no one knew what the new tax laws were going to be, no one knew when the markets were going to grow again. And I'll never forget this part; she said, "I'm not going to invest money in my company until I know what the future looks like."

The panel started arguing that point with her, and like so many times before, the debate became unwatchable as each person tried to yell louder than the other. I stopped watching, but the comments started to really sink in. This business owner wanted a sure thing in the economy, government, and marketplace. Here was a business owner on a national television program saying essentially, "My business isn't worth my time or my money."

It sounded like something you would hear from an investor analyzing the financials and the market before deciding if a business venture was a worthy investment, not a business owner. Where was her passion? More importantly, where was the vision? Obviously this owner was focused on the obstacles in front of her and not on any opportunities that might exist.

This is a classic example of an entrepreneur who transformed into just a business owner. Instead of growth, she was looking for consistency. Rather than taking a risk, she wanted a stable return on her investment. I don't know her; in fact, I don't even remember where she was from or what business she represented. I just remember the words and the feelings it stirred up in me. It made me think she had already given up.

Deciding to be comfortable with change is not the easiest thing in the world. Most people are more comfortable in a stable, consistent environment. But that isn't the reality of a small business. Things change all the time. You have to be ready to react to a change in the market or a change in your customer's wants or needs. In the beginning this is much easier. But as your business matures, you have more to lose. Focusing on maintenance rather than on growth will stall your momentum and, eventually, your business.

Building adaptability into your culture is one of the cornerstones of business growth. Don't fool yourself into thinking it's an easy thing to do. There are a lot of challenges you will have to face, but the end result is a healthier, stronger company.

The first major challenge comes from marketing. Most of the training that is available will talk about finding your niche or developing your core. They are all ways of saying the same thing—identify whom you are going to serve and what you are going to do to serve them. Easy, right? The problem is, people's needs change. The market changes; technology changes. What was your core last year isn't needed as much this year and won't exist in five years. To be successful you have to learn how to be nimble with your ideas and forceful with your actions.

I've seen several business owners turn down opportunities because they said it wasn't a part of their "core" business offering. Be careful when making these types of decisions. Not having a wide enough view of your market and your customers' changing needs can leave you with an outdated company that no longer solves a problem your market experiences.

Think about a payroll company. They may believe their core is processing payroll checks for clients. The training they receive is heavily focused on payroll law and tax filing requirements. They differentiate themselves by processing checks faster and more accurately than the competition. But eventually a customer is going to ask them to process other types of payments. Maybe it is the withholding payments to various insurance companies, or maybe it's payments to a retirement plan or something else all together.

This business must make a choice about their future. A business owner is going to evaluate the costs of expanding, the risks of new services, and the potential long-term growth of the revenue. *Is this our core? Do we want to go outside what we do best? Is this the business I want?*

A business owner with a growth mentality is going to look at this and decide on a course of action that will grow the business. He or she may look at the market and decide payroll processing is dying out. It's all automated with direct deposit and pay cards. Checks are obsolete. In order to grow, the business must adapt. Are you ready to take on that challenge when it is your business model that has become obsolete?

There are six keys to developing a culture of adaptability:

- Consistently build your skills.
- Embrace technology.
- Emphasize speed.
- Act without certainty.
- Develop market awareness.
- Solve problems.

In order for your business to grow, you have to grow, too! Even in companies that have a strong training and continuing education program, the business owner seems to be left out. Make sure you are developing your own skills.

Attend training regularly, but not just in your field. Look at similar industries, and start learning what works well for them. You aren't looking for a mastery of these other fields, but look for tips and suggestions that might help you and your business. One of the easiest ways to solve a problem is to look to others who already have a solution. Get in the habit of seeking out unusual and creative answers to problems.

Read on a regular basis. In fact, take a look at your bookshelf. What is the quality of the books you have at your fingertips? It's amazing what twenty bucks and a few hours can do for your business. Magazines, articles, blogs, newspapers, and journals can be great resources as well. But pay attention to the quality of the content. Try to read high-quality materials at least thirty minutes each day. Make it a habit. If you need to, block out the time in your schedule just like a regular meeting.

There are hundreds of ways to improve your skills, but the important thing is to commit to it. Take a class. Enroll in a training program. Buy books—and read them. Find what works for you and then do it. Once you've developed a skill, though, there is one more thing you need to do.

Teach.

Write it down, create a presentation, or stand up and do a speech. But you have to teach what you learn. The only way the training will stick with you is to apply it. As the leader of your company, the best way to apply your new skills is to teach them to others. You will also show your employees through your actions how much you value self-improvement and training. Once you set the example, hold the rest of your team accountable to developing their skills.

Next, focus on the technology in your business. Using technology is not enough. Embrace it. Develop a hunger for technology. Every day it seems we are being shown some new advancement in computers, software, or smart phones. Technology can increase productivity. It can speed up your response times. It can keep your teams in contact and on task. Of course, there are disadvantages to technology, but they don't outweigh the benefits. I hear it often: "We want to provide a personal touch to our customers." This is the argument against technology. What it usually tells me is that the business is either too cheap, too old school, or too afraid of technology to use it correctly.

Technology is the great equalizer in business. I can open an online retail store in less than a day and offer the same products you can find in a traditional bricks-and-mortar store. My online retail store doesn't require a building, and if I do it right, it doesn't require inventory. I can partner up with a warehouse that ships the items directly to the customer, and all I have to worry about is my Web site. Oh, and I use a program that allows me to point and click to build the site. No programming required. Technology. Think I'm exaggerating? When was the last time you walked into an Amazon store?

There is a big difference between buying the latest and greatest computer and using technology in your business. Buying the latest and greatest is nice for the people using the computers, but it doesn't make your business hi-tech! Using technology means that you are creating solutions using a wide variety of channels.

Really focus in on how the software in your company is being used. Many industries rely on software programs to enter customer data, process reports, fulfill orders, communicate with clients, and so much more. But in most cases, the software that a company purchases to handle these functions is not utilized fully. Make sure you get the most out of every solution you bring into your company.

Technology can change your employment base as well. Managers and accountants tend to look at technology as a way to cut payroll costs. "Replace our customer-service people with an automated answering service, and we'll save thousands of dollars" is how the thinking usually goes. For me, that is a waste of technology and manpower. Use technology to enhance your offering and change the duties of your workforce. Instead of having a team of customer-service agents, utilize them in marketing and sales. Remember the goal is business growth, not cost cutting.

Also be mindful of your customer experience. While technology can increase what services are available to your customers, it can't replace a real, live person. If you are trying to provide a personal touch in your customer experience, take that into consideration as you incorporate technology into your company.

Don't be afraid of technology. Some people just are not and will never be technically savvy. If you are one of those people, that's fine. But don't let it affect your business. Surround yourself with trusted advisors. Talk to industry experts, and learn what is needed. Then hold your teams account-able to delivering it. Don't feel like you have to become a technical wizard in order to keep up.

Technology will help you with the next step, which is moving with speed. Starting projects is the easy part; finishing them makes people struggle. When I'm working with a group of people on projects, the first thing I do is draw a straight horizontal line and make a tick mark about halfway through. I'll point to the tick mark and tell them, "Before we can finish this project, we have to get to the halfway point." I'll draw another tick mark between the first one and the end of the line. "Once there, we still have to get halfway again." I'll keep repeating this process until all they can see is a lump of dashes at the end of the line.

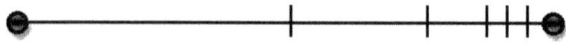

This certainly isn't a new idea. But sometimes a team needs to see it drawn out. Think of the tick marks as obstacles to projects. As you get closer and closer to the end of any project, these obstacles will show up more frequently. Resources start to become scarce, commitment levels fall, disagreements about how the final product will look crop up, and dead-lines start to get missed. Finishing projects is hard work.

It is why you need to value speed in your organization. Quick deci-sions, quick actions, quick results. Look at how your employees interact with their work now. Are there built-in delays? Is there too much bureau-cracy between the people on the front lines and those in charge of making decisions?

Focus on making it easy for employees to react quickly to a changing workplace. Eliminate redundant processes that slow down the work. Look for ways to reduce the time your employees must spend on their tasks. Use technology to help speed up processes. The time your employees spend on unnecessary steps stalls the momentum of your company. If a front-line employee notices a problem that needs to be addressed, does he have the authority to make the change? How many levels of management or deci-sion makers need to provide input before the company can put in a new service?

When you do have projects in place, prepare to add resources closer to the deadline. Don't change the leader or the scope of the project; just add resources. Adding extra money, extra manpower, extra software, or whatever else is needed at the right time will speed up projects. Remember, one completed project is worth hundreds of started and never finished projects.

Organizations that are in constant motion find it easier to adapt to changes in the market. Develop a monthly meeting where your employees can share any ideas or thoughts they have had about the direction of your market. It's one thing for you to try to gather this information alone, but having your entire work force committed to learning about the marketplace is powerful. Your accounting team will be talking to your vendors each month. Your customer-service team will be talking to your customers each month. Your sales and marketing teams will be talking to prospects and researching the competition each month. With just a little change in focus, each of these teams could be collecting valuable data each month about your market and positioning your company as a leader. During the meeting, each department can share what they have learned and discuss any trends or opportunities that may be visible.

You are constantly learning. Technology is running rampant through your company. Decisions and actions are moving at light speed. You know everything about your market. Now what? Focus on providing solutions!

We've talked a lot about creating products and services that solve problems in the market. It's the only way you can capture a niche and make consistent sales. But here we are going to talk about solving internal problems as a way to help your business grow.

As the business owner, you are asked to wear many hats: leader, decision maker, salesperson, manager, investor, employee, and on and on. But you are uniquely positioned as the only person in your company who can make the final decision on everything. That fact alone means the most important thing you can do is provide answers and solutions when your teams are faced with change.

Too often employees and managers get bogged down in the details and negativity of the work they are doing. They see all the obstacles to change and decide the status quo is better or at the very least safer. They can't see beyond the short-term pain of the change your company must make in order to stay competitive. You need to use your status as the business owner to clear whatever roadblocks your employees, managers, customers, the markets, the government, and anyone else can come up with to derail your plans. If you allow yourself to see the obstacles, too, your company will stop adapting and become extinct.

There are times when a person in authority will let others make mistakes as a way to help teach independence. No one wants to be in a position where every little problem needs management approval. Experience is a cruel but fair teacher. The test may come first, but the lesson sticks with you much longer. But there is a time when you can sit back and let your employees learn things on their own, and this isn't it.

When your company is in the middle of growth and change, you need to be ready to answer questions directly and honestly. Give your team all the information they need, and then give them a little more so they can get the work done. Provide immediate solutions to problems as they come up. Don't wait for someone else to figure it out. Be the leader who steps up and leads your team into the next phase of your company. Don't sit back and be a backseat driver complaining about what everyone else is doing and offering nothing useful. Solve their problems, and they'll build out the new processes you need to keep serving your customers.

Change is never easy to deal with, but remember, you chose a life of uncertainty when you decided to start your own company. Don't shy away from it now. If you want stability and comfort, close your doors and go get a job. Otherwise create an environment that embraces uncertainty and change, and seek out new opportunities for your business to grow.

22

When Will I Ever Be Able To Step Back And Let My Business Support Me Instead Of The Other Way Around?

When You Stop Pretending To Be A Business Owner.

I've been asked this question in a lot of different ways:

- I'm ready to sell this business; how do I make it look better to investors?
- I want to retire next year; how do I get my business ready to continue on without me?
- I want to take a vacation with my family, but my business needs me; what do I do?
- I never see my family anymore; how can I cut my workday from fifteen hours to ten?
- I need a day off, but how can I keep this place from falling apart while I'm gone?

I have the same answer for all of them. If you are asking this question, then it will never happen. You have to build every aspect of your business with this goal in mind. Starting now is too late, but we can start putting the pieces in place now so you can build to that moment when you can step back and start acting like a business owner and stop being an employee.

Most business owners I talk to get offended when I tell them they aren't acting like real business owners. The least secure ones are even more offended when I call them employees. (These business owners are also more likely to have employees who hate them!) But in the end, the fact remains: if your business can't function without you there, then you haven't created a business for yourself; you've created a job instead.

Employees trade hours for dollars. If they are very lucky, they will find someone willing to pay them enough per hour so they can pay their bills and have a little leftover. Some of them will use that leftover money to invest and carve out a little retirement. Most of them will use that leftover money to buy new toys and create more debt, forcing them to continue looking for new ways to get more money. This is the trap of the employee mindset. The only way they can build wealth is to either get more per hour or to work more hours.

Investors trade money for more money—or at least they try to. Investors spend time researching an opportunity and look for ways to make their own money grow. If they are lucky, they will find lightning in a bottle and invest in a product or company that takes off. If they are reckless, they will throw their money away on the next greatest flop. Either way, the money investors make or lose has nothing to do with the number of hours they work. It is simply about the skills and diligence they have to make wise decisions and take calculated risks.

As a small-business owner, your business is a large part of your net worth. One of your goals is to build your business so that you can enjoy the benefits of added wealth. But what does building wealth mean? Most businesses are able to get by month to month just paying the bills and keeping the doors open. But is that what a successful business really feels like? You may be building value in your business by staying open, but is that the same thing as building wealth? Growing your business and tapping into the power of momentum is about creating a business that does more than just pay the bills. If you are reading this book, you have an interest in building something better than what you currently have. To build wealth, your business must acquire or create assets that provide consistent, recurring revenue.

Business owners are investors who have decided to invest their money into themselves. Rather than betting on any other business to grow their money, they have decided their business, their idea, their effort, their vision, and their work ethic will provide the greatest return. I mean, that's exactly what you thought of when you opened your doors, right?

Actually, most people who own their own business get into it because they enjoy the work and feel like they can make some money at it, maybe even more than they could get working for someone else. In other words, they open their business with an employee mindset. Rather than trading hours for money with an employer, they are going to trade hours for money with their customers. So in terms of generating a business that will pay you long term, what have you really created? Nothing.

You have a business that is entirely dependent on you. If you don't work, or provide services, you aren't getting paid. So you hire a few employees to do some of the work for you. But now you need more customers to pay your employees and yourself. So you hire more salespeople, and the process repeats. Get big enough, and the difficulty of everything multiplies—employee relations, client acquisition and service, billing and payables, payroll, legal, and on and on. At some point every business owner looks back and thinks being in business would be simpler if it was just a one-person show again.

I worked with a company that was headed up by two partners. They were good friends and had run their business for quite some time without any major battles between them. Their company had started to stall, and they were struggling to get things back on track. Talking with them together, they seemed to be on the same page and ready to make whatever changes they needed in order to get the company moving in the right direction.

Separately, though, it was a different story. Each of them had an idea of what they wanted the company to look like going forward. One wanted to keep the company small, become more efficient, and control costs. The other wanted to grow the company fast—more locations, more customers, more employees, and more profits. They started to resent each other over it, and the company was suffering because they couldn't get on the same page. In the end, they ended up dissolving the partnership.

The point is, be clear about what you want your business to look like. Do you want a big business with all of its complexities, or do you want something smaller with the uncertainty of how to continue to build your revenue? If you are conflicted about what you want your business to be, you will end up like this partnership. Everything you do to take a step forward will turn into several steps backward when you change your mind.

After you know whether you want to own a big business or a small business, the rest becomes pretty straightforward. You have to change your mindset from employee to business owner. You have to think of your business as an investment. And just like any investment, it has to be high quality, low risk, and give you back more money than you put into it. The two most important things you can do to increase the value of your investment is hire the best talent you can find and develop as many passive income streams as possible.

One of the most important things an investor looks at is the quality of the management team. Does the team have the knowledge, experience, and skills that are needed to be successful in their industry? Is past performance a result of the work of the management team or just plain old-fashioned blind luck?

Luck is not something you invest in. There is a little town in the Nevada desert that has monuments built on the backs of those who invested in their own luck. Don't get caught up in the luck of your business—good or bad.

Get in the habit of measuring everything. If you have a great month or quarter, figure out what action you or your team took to generate that success. Did you introduce a new product or service? Did you start a new marketing campaign? Were you able to cut costs? When you are able to tie the performance of your company to the decisions of your management team, then you know you aren't dealing with luck.

But what happens if you can't tie them together? Well first of all, make sure you have a system in place to measure these results. As an investor, you need data. If your company can't produce the information you need to make better decisions, then you need to fix that problem right away. But if you are getting the information and it seems like nothing your management team does affects your business performance, then you need to make a change. Your business is your investment. It's your income now, and your retirement income in the future. If it doesn't have the highest-quality parts and pieces, then you are putting your entire investment at risk. Don't be afraid to hire the highest-quality people you can find. Yes, it is going to cost more to bring these people in. But the benefits far outweigh the costs. You need a management team that is going to grow your business and provide you with independence. Hiring cheap idiots won't get you there.

And one other thing, don't hire or promote anyone based on potential. It's a fool's trap. You will always end up waiting for that potential to be reached, and you'll hold on to a bad hire longer because you get invested in his or her future success. Build your team on proven skills and prior accomplishments. Don't chase down dreams.

When you have a team that knows what it's doing, is skilled at producing results, and can handle the growth of your business, you won't feel the need to be at the office every hour of every day. And it'll happen all of a sudden. You'll walk in one day and see everyone working hard for you. You'll look at a few reports, ask a few questions, and realize all the hard work is being done by someone else. In fact, you may start to feel a little sad that your company doesn't need you as much anymore. All that extra time you were looking for doesn't seem as important now that it is staring you in the face. You might even start thinking you miss working in your business.

But don't give in to that feeling! You are an investor. This is what success feels like. Now you have time to find another investment and to enjoy all the things you passed up to get this business moving forward. You have now created a stream of passive income, and for true financial freedom, you need to get more.

Passive income streams are what every business owner and investor are looking for. They are the difference between living paycheck to paycheck and being financially free for life. Passive income is wealth that comes in without regards to the time or effort you put out. Right now you are holding one of my passive income generators. Every time someone buys this book, I get a royalty. Which is way better than writing this book every time someone placed an order.

If you truly want to step back from your business, then you need to find ways to create passive income in your life and in your business. One of the quickest passive income generators is real estate. Buy a building and rent it out. The rent money comes in based on the number of tenants, not the number of hours you work. This is one of the reasons so many business owners own their building and lease it back to their business. Instant passive income for the owner!

Real estate might be the most recognized industry when we discuss this formula. Owning your home is an investment. But it's not a way that you would build wealth. In order to build true wealth, you would want to have properties that generate revenue. So instead of just owning your home, you would need to own a house that you are able to rent out. You would create wealth based on the number of properties you own and how much cash they generate from rent beyond your costs to purchase and maintain them.

Each building you own would be valued by the rent it produces. Multi-unit properties can generate more rental income so they have a higher value. Think of it like this. Given the choice, would you rather own a single-family home or a duplex as a rental property? The duplex allows you to get two sources of income to help pay any of your costs. It is a better asset to hold on to because it is building your wealth faster.

Now apply this to your business. What types of products and services do you offer? How well does each item generate revenue for your business? How do you look at your products and services? Are you holding them to the same standard you would a rental property? Are they building wealth for your business?

Don't get stuck thinking like an employee when it comes to passive income. I can hear it already: "My business doesn't have a way to generate passive income." Yeah right. Every business can do it. The question is, are you ready to think like an investor in your business? Are you ready to make finding passive sources of income a priority?

Beyond real estate there are several other ways to create passive income in your business. The most popular and effective way is through exclusive memberships. Think of country clubs and gyms. Every month you pay a fee for access to a facility or resources. This fee isn't based on your actual use. You pay it either way. So how can you add something like that to your business? Maybe you offer a small annual fee to your customers so they can get exclusive training, content, sales promotions, or some other perk. The recurring revenue to you happens without any additional effort or billable hours, and it can be repeated over and over with all of your customers.

Get creative and think of ways to boost your revenue with passive income generators. When you talk about having your business work for you, passive income is going to be the difference maker. Business owners who know how to develop these programs are light years ahead of everyone else in the race to a comfortable, early retirement.

23

I've got it all figured out.

"We Have To Give Them The Pickle."

Whether it comes across or not, I have a tremendous respect for people who make the decision to start their own business. It takes a little crazy to make that choice, and I've learned many times over you don't mess with crazy. So as I was writing this book, I made every attempt to treat the material and the reader with respect. But then I was reminded of something else. Most of the business owners I've met don't have a friggin' clue about what they are doing.

Nothing reminds me of that more than the story of the pickle.

I was doing some work for a small service firm. They had been in business over fifteen years and had built up a decent following. For the first few years, they were the only game in town. They grew quickly and established a strong reputation in the community. Their only real competition was from national chains that didn't have a strong presence in this community. After a while, a few small shops opened up around town, but there was enough business that no one really had a problem getting customers. Everyone was able to grow his or her business without worrying about each other.

But as the community grew, the market became more competitive. The national chains started to take notice of the growth and decided to expand their presence. With these new competitors, it became obvious the market wasn't big enough to support them all, so everyone starting targeting each others' customers. For the first time in this company's history, they were having to really work to get new clients and were struggling to hold on to the ones they already had. There was a lot of stress in the office, but we were working toward a new plan.

This business owner had some unusual habits, but nothing too far out of the ordinary. He was a little rough around the edges in how he dealt with people, but overall he was a good guy. I had been working with him and his sales manager on a strategy to improve their overall community image. The biggest problem we had identified was that they were established. It seemed like everyone wanted to try something new, which is why they were having trouble holding on to their business. We couldn't find service issues, the pricing was in line with the market, and the services were high quality even if they were a little stale.

One day, as the sales manager and I were working through lunch, we heard the business owner bellowing throughout the office. "We're going to give them the pickle!" It was loud. The office walls echoed his words. Three times he shouted it. "Will, where are you? We're going to give them the pickle!"

I got him into the office we were using, and he had the biggest grin on his face. "Will, I've got it all figured out. We're going to give them the pickle!" Obviously I had a very confused look on my face because I didn't say a word, but he continued to explain.

"I was at lunch, and that's when it hit me. They delivered my sandwich and chips to my table. And right there next to my sandwich was a pickle. I didn't order it; I didn't even ask for it. But they gave it to me anyway. It's like everything we've been talking about. We have to give them something so they'll know we care."

It wasn't a great analogy, but it certainly inspired him so we went with it. The sales manager nodded slightly then asked him quietly to not mention the pickle anymore. It didn't work. The business owner left the little room we were in, walked up to every employee, and with a big grin on his face said, "We're going to give them the pickle!"

Of course, every employee in that building was female. Sexual innuendoes aside, it had to be the most ridiculous thing for the staff to hear.

No one was impressed. A few of the younger girls giggled with each other later. Others were a little offended by it. I heard later that his office manager told him there were a few complaints about it so he apologized for disrupting their work.

In the end, the pickle strategy never developed. It became a running joke in the office, but it was never considered a serious long term strategy. It's a shame. The idea behind it was sound. Giving value when and where it isn't expected tends to be well received by customers. If it had been communicated any other way besides "giving them the pickle" it just might have had a chance.

I refer to it every now and again as the pickle story. It's a reminder to me that too many business owners think they have it all figured out. It's also a reminder that even the best ideas can fail if they are communicated poorly. But more than that, it's a reminder of just how clueless business owners can be about how their actions affect others.

Growth isn't an accident. It is the result of careful planning and a focus and commitment to making it all work. We need business owners who are willing to take chances and grow their businesses. We need innovation to create new markets and new opportunities for the next generation of workers. It's only through a strong small-business community that our economy can thrive. There isn't any great, mystical secret to business success. You need a product or service you can sell for more than it costs you to produce. Sell enough of it, and you get a profit. Sell more and you can retire. Easy.

Fixing businesses is the easy part; fixing business owners is where it gets tricky.

It's why I wrote this book.

About The Author

As a consultant, speaker, and author, William J. Eisenbrandt has spent the past several years helping small-business owners grow their businesses in an uncertain economy. He uses his management experience in the retail, insurance, finance, employee relations, and technology industries to develop his unique style with a strong emphasis on obtaining results. With multiple degrees and certifications in the fields of business, accounting, and finance and a firm belief that knowledge is something to be shared, Eisenbrandt enjoys every opportunity to teach what he's observed, what he's learned, and, occasionally, what he thinks. Eisenbrandt is the founder of Vertical Business Group, a business consulting and management firm that is dedicated to providing small businesses the services and support they need to grow and succeed. He currently lives in the Pacific Northwest with his wife and son.

www.ingramcontent.com/pod-product-compliance
Lightning Source LLC
Chambersburg PA
CBHW061507180526
45171CB00001B/72